Inside Project Red Stripe

Incubating Innovation and Teamwork at *The Economist*

Andrew Carey

Published in this first edition in 2008 by:
Triarchy Press
Station Offices
Axminster
Devon. EX13 5PF
United Kingdom

+44 (0)1297 631456
info@triarchypress.com
www.triarchypress.com

A catalogue record for this book is available from the British Library.

Cover design and image by Heather Fallows -
www.whitespacegallery.org.uk

ISBN: 978-0-9550081-6-0

Online edition: www.projectredstripe.blogspot.com

DRAMATIS PERSONÆ

STEVEN CHIU,

STEWART ROBINSON,

MIKE SEERY,

                                 the Project Red Stripe team

TOM SHELLEY,

LUDWIG SIEGELE,

JOANNA SLYKERMAN,

HELEN ALEXANDER, *chief executive of The Economist Group*

JAVIER BAJER, *coach to the team*

SALLY BIBB,

GERARD FAIRTLOUGH,   *occasional consultants to the team*

DAVID LAIRD,

THE GMC, *The Economist Group's Group Management Committee*

BECOMING-WHALE-OF-AN-IDEA, *an overweening creature*

OFFSTAGE, *manifold other experts, idea-contributors, colleagues, designers, blogorati, technorati, board-level executives and such like, too numerous to mention except in an Oscars' acceptance speech.*

SCENE: *London, The Marylebone Road; Sunningdale Park, The National School of Government*

Timeline

2006

April –   The Economist Group's 'Internet Strategy Group' discusses ways of improving the Group's presence on the Internet. Mike Seery, the CIO, suggests an internally recruited team and is asked to put a proposal to the Group Management Committee (GMC).

June –   The GMC is generally supportive, but there is concern about damaging the brand and about the financial cost. Approval given for Mike to recruit a team of five people plus himself from within the Group, remove them from their current jobs, and give them £100,000 and six months to develop and launch an innovative product, service or business model on the web.

September –   Mike hosts three webcasts, attended by about 120 Economist Group employees.

October –   21 people submit web-based applications to join the team.

News of Project Red Stripe – 'The Economist's new digital incubation unit' – is reported on PaidContent.org (the leading blog/website on 'digital content' and the publishing industry).

December –   After a bout of flu and lengthy discussions with their managers, Mike announces the other five team members.

2007

January

29th –   Project Red Stripe begins

February –   Team building exercises, team orientation and idea sharing. Discussion of the crowdsourcing exercise and making plans for a prototype process and then the 'real thing'.

March –   Most of the month is devoted to reading, sifting and evaluating the ideas received from the crowdsourcing process.

9th –	The crowdsourcing goes live (the prototype and real thing are merged into one process).
11th –	The call for ideas is featured on slashdot.org
25th –	Closing date for the idea-gathering process.
April –	Researching, discussing, arguing, clarifying what the idea should be, more researching.
23rd –	Presentation of **Project Bavaria** (universal primary education idea) to Gerard Fairtlough.
May –	Development of **Lughenjo** (eventually a philanthropy social exchange/network and website), online research, discussions with *Economist* colleagues, technology partners and experts in the field. Preparing marketing plan and business plan. Evolution from a not-for-profit into a commercial business. Web site planning and development.
June –	Work on **Lughenjo** website, research and discussion with partners, charities, NGOs, etc.
14th –	Presentation of **Project Lughenjo** to the GMC.
29th –	The team goes public with the **Lughenjo** idea and invites feedback.
July	
Weeks 1/2 –	Talking to social entrepreneurs and NGOs. **Lughenjo** evolves into a social/knowledge network ('codenamed' **HiSpace**) for *The Economist* target market, with philanthropy and business travel as just two of its potential components.
20th –	Presentation of **HiSpace** social networking idea to the GMC.
28th –	Project Red Stripe ends. Mike continues to work alone on **HiSpace**.
30th –	PaidContent.org reports: '*Economist* Innovation Project Ends Without A Product; Community Idea In "Cold Storage"'.

August –   Mike Seery publishes *Project Red Stripe: A Story of Innovation*, with an account of the project and recommendations for future innovation teams.

December

17th –   PaidContent.org reports: '*Economist* Ready To Try "Social Networking" Again' as publishing director Ben Edwards says a new conversation portal for "incredibly bright and influential people" is in the early stages of development.

2008

Spring –   **HiSpace** is mothballed as a stand-alone business idea because, in a nutshell, The Economist Group isn't worried enough about the current business model to want to invest heavily in the new one.

Changes to the Economist.com website (blogs, reader participation, etc.) start to reflect some of the paths and possibilities discussed (and rejected as too obvious or incremental) by the Red Stripe team a year earlier. Chicken or egg?

Becoming-Whale

Stewart: *'There was a problem with us not being able to pick an outcome.'*

Herman Melville's Moby-Dick 'is not like the little cat or dog owned by an elderly woman who honors and cherishes it'. He is no ordinary whale. In the same vein, Project Red Stripe's big idea, whatever it was to be, was not like the kind of idea that you have in the bath.

Of course, it could have been an idea that you have in the bath. But it wasn't, because it quickly acquired a weight and a symbolism and a significance that transformed it into something quite other. So that having it in the bath would have been as improbable as having Moby-Dick in the bath.

Moby-Dick was no ordinary whale but one that 'bypasse[d] the pack or the school'; less an animal than an event in its own right and one whose character and fleshiness are partly an emergent property of Ahab's relationship with the whale. Another emergent property (or side-effect, as we used to say) of that relationship was that the captain ceased to be just Ahab. Choosing to hunt Moby-Dick 'in a choosing that exceeds him and comes from elsewhere', Ahab is eventually overtaken by his preoccupation with the beast. He can be seen as 'becoming-whale'. So Red Stripe's idea, whatever it was to be, was no ordinary idea. And the team can be seen as becoming-idea.

Taking the notion of Ahab-becoming-whale one step further, we could also imagine that, in the course of Ahab's struggle with it, the whale somehow changes. Perhaps Moby-Dick is himself becoming-more-than-whale. He is becoming-Ahab. So the idea can be seen as becoming-the-team.

In any case, a sense of the idea (though not the idea itself) was there in Mike Seery's head nine months before the project began when he proposed an internal innovation team to the Internet Strategy Group, of which he was a member.

Though he tried to talk it away – 'the key measure of success is not the idea itself, but that The Economist Group wants to run this innovation process again' – it continued to preoccupy him. The idea of an idea. 'It should be something that we couldn't otherwise have come up with.' It also preoccupied the team from the outset. Where would they find it? Would they know it when they saw it? Would they catch it? Would they be good enough for it? Would it be good enough for them? Would it be cool enough? Would they deserve it? If they found it, would other people recognise it? Would someone else steal it once they'd found it?

As Mike said later about the idea-gathering process:

> ... by the time each team member had read through all of the ideas and the rush of new submissions had turned into a trickle, we knew that we still lacked the big idea. And we were already nearly two months into the project.

To me it seems that this whale-of-an-idea was sometimes too much for the team. Too much for any team. They tried to bring it back down to size by playing with it: 'Let's divert the Thames through Lichfield', 'Let's make the world square'. But still it became the elephant in the room, to mix gargantuan mammal metaphors. And the team found themselves becoming-whale-of-an-idea-in-the-room. Then they had two ideas. Which one should they choose? Had they chosen the right idea? Then the idea was altered. Was it still good enough? Then it was changed altogether. As time ran out there was an awful dread that they had missed their chance. And, from the moment that they decided to look externally for their idea, there was a pervading sense that the idea lived 'out there'. Which meant, in turn, that the team would not be the authors or creators or owners of the idea.

In the end, it's a serious responsibility being invited to change the world. The whale-of-an-idea is an onerous beastie, and cetanthropy is an onerous business.

Dilemmas:

- 'Thinking big' is obviously necessary for a major innovation project, especially as it's notoriously difficult to get people to think beyond the confines of their current reality. But giving people the freedom to try and change the world may leave them a little dazed by the enormity of what they might be able to achieve.

Notes – Becoming-Whale

- **Meta-Note**
  Since this book is intended for online and print publication, it needs both conventional endnotes and bibliography as well as hyperlinking. This is more problematic than it seems, if you want to keep the text more or less identical in both versions (for ease of cross referencing). Certainly it's easier to follow the references to different chapters in this book and to external sources if you can follow the hyperlinks online. But I've also tried to ensure that everything is suitably annotated for the paper reader.

  One convention I should explain concerns links to external sources. In the first note below, for example, I have given a conventional page reference to a title listed in the **Bibliography** [Deleuze & Guattari, 1987]. However, the hyperlink in the online edition (at www. projectredstripe.blogspot.com) leads not to the **Bibliography** but to a full text extract from the book on Google Book Search. Equally, later in the same note, the conventional reference is to Lise Lavelle's published PhD thesis [Lavelle, 2006] but the hyperlink is to a website which gives a brief introduction to Lavelle's work (but not the full thesis).

- The quotations are all from [Deleuze & Guattari, 1987: 268-9], whose particular interest is in context: the inseparability of the individual human from the surrounding environment – which is at the heart of their discourse on rhizome, networks and nets. This, in turn, connects to the discussion of weaving in **Drifting, Angst and Pan-ic** (page 29) and to Sandra Reeve's emphasis on the inescapable interlinking of the individual, other people and the environment (discussed in **Creative Compartments**, page 151).

- If all this seems far removed from the world of business and innovation, have a look at 'Other Work' [Bäckius, 2002], which effortlessly links Cicero, Deleuze, Peter Drucker, Tom Peters, Foucault, Nietzsche and Luhmann.

- Mike's earlier remarks were made in a conversation I had with him just before the project started. The longer extract is from the report that he wrote after the Project finished [Seery, 2007].

- Cetanthropy is my neologism, following the suggestion of lycanthropy (werewolfery). Google has no results for it (yet) and politely suggests that I might have intended 'Stanthorpe'.

- Meta-dilemma: at Gerard Fairtlough's suggestion, I've added a list of dilemmas at the end of most chapters (to highlight the main points covered in that chapter). Inevitably, there's room for considerable duplication as many of the same issues raise their heads in different ways and at different times during the course of the project and the book. Should I repeat them? In the end I have – on the grounds that, if you notice the same dilemma two or three times, it's likely to be a significant one for your own team.

How Not to Read This Book

On my way home from my first meeting with Mike Seery, I was thinking about writing this book. I had already concluded that I would be observing and writing about the team as an anthropologist.

I would be in the rare position of observing a team at work, in a real business situation, under potentially extreme pressure, without having to do anything. I wasn't there in the role of facilitator or consultant or psychologist. I didn't have to look for anything in particular, report back or make recommendations. I didn't have to do anything that was intended to change the group. And because I wasn't paid by the team or the team's employers, I was also not beholden to anyone for anything.

Coincidentally, I had just attended a lecture by anthropologist Professor Tim Ingold, in which he'd neatly summarised the recent history of anthropology. With the advent of relativism and the abandonment of the notion that Western, white culture was in any sense more advanced than that of its neighbours, anthropologists had had to stop making judgements about the people they observed.

With the advent of post-modernism, anthropologists had further lost confidence in their ability to offer an objective account of life as lived by the people they were observing (partly, at least, because the language, culture, environment and lived experience of their hosts were so alien that no real understanding of them would ever be possible). All that was left to the anthropologist was to write about her own experience of living among these people and to record her own inner process.

So, I thought, if I wasn't going to make judgements about the rightness or wrongness of the way the team approached the project, I would have to write about something. As a result, on my first visit to the team, I made a list of some of the things I could pay attention to:

- What's on the walls
- What stories and jokes they tell each other
- How they have fun
- How they deal with difficulties and irritations
- What happens outside the office
- What language they use
- How they sit and move about
- How I feel when I'm there

Which may help to explain the approach I've taken to writing this book. I subsequently also found some justification for this approach when reading Humberto Maturana, who said:

> When one puts objectivity in parenthesis, all views, all verses in the multiverse are equally valid. Understanding this, you lose the passion for changing the other. One of the results is that you look apathetic to people. Now, those who do not live with objectivity in parentheses have a passion for changing the other. So they have this passion and you do not... And I think that this is the main difficulty. To other people you may seem too tolerant. However, if the others also put objectivity in parentheses, you discover that disagreements can only be solved by entering a domain of co-inspiration, in which things are done together because the participants want to do them. With objectivity in parentheses, it is easy to do things together because one is not denying the other in the process of doing them.

I took this as my starting point in observing the team and take it here as my point of reference whenever I feel tempted to make a recommendation based on my experience of the team. With this in mind, I have tried to report what I saw and heard and felt, to ask some questions and introduce some 'verses', to co-opt Maturana's term. Judgements I shall leave to others. That means not saying where I thought something was good or bad. But one judgement I cannot resist. I could not have done better than these people and I rather doubt that any other group could have done better either. They have my respect and admiration. They are also lovely people.

As well as avoiding judgements, I had another concern. Returning from a visit to Project Red Stripe on 19th June, 2007, I read the following in a review of *The Black Swan: The impact of the highly improbable* by Nassim Nicholas Taleb:

> *Taleb feels... that humans naturally distort facts through their natural love of narrative. They can't help but make up causal stories to explain the sheer randomness of things.*

Historians, policemen, sociologists, neuroscientists, psychologists and anthropologists all rightly doubt the human capacity to combine narrative story telling with factual accuracy.

So how, as a self-proclaimed organisational anthropologist, was I to do any better? How to avoid putting one fact in front of another, one recollection after another? How to avoid the craving to offer: 'this happened because they did this'?

One way is to avoid a chronological narrative – which explains why the order of the remaining chapters is rather arbitrary. So, please feel free to choose your own path through the text and dip in and out at will. For anyone who wants detailed references or who wants to pursue the different trains of thought that emerge, the notes to each chapter should help, but the hyperlinks in the online version offer the primrosiest path. There's also a kind of index of ideas, here:

Index of ideas

(Each of the listed themes – shown in bold – features in the chapters listed beneath it. Page references for the chapters appear in italics.)

Corporate Innovation/Intrapreneurship

Hierarchy

Theories of Innovation, Business and Teams:

Success/Failure

Psychometric Profiling

The Project Red Stripe Team Story

Useful Questions, Methods and Ideas for Teams and Innovation Teams

Furthermore, as a historian (once upon a time), I'm aware that an old-fashioned approach to writing about Project Red Stripe would have focused on the personalities of the actors; that a modern one would emphasise the social, organisational and economic forces at work on the team; that yet another would examine the processes used or the techniques (for example, of conflict-resolution) that were deployed; that a Sengean one would stress the 'presence' of the individual team members and their energy (itself an emergent property of their presence, attention and focus); and that a postmodern one would bang on about semiotics and becoming-whale until you rolled over and lost the will to live. So I have tried to combine them all and to allow you to choose your own preferred perspective.

Even further more, let's return to Taleb, who is a hedge fund manager. He maintains that all the conventional market and financial indicators are irrelevant to the trader, because everyone else is already accounting for them. In effect, he says that we can't know why stock markets go up and down – we just make up post hoc explanations. I suspect the same is true of innovation projects – another reason for me not to pile yet more 'how to do innovation' prescriptions onto the mountain of 'how to do innovation' guides already out there. For the same reason, instead of conventional bullet-pointed lists of 'tips', you'll find dilemmas highlighted at the end of some chapters. These are dilemmas that the Red Stripe team faced and which other innovation projects are also likely to face – so, if you're involved in an innovation project yourself, it's perhaps worth giving them some thought beforehand.

Dilemmas

- With sufficient detachment, it becomes impossible to reach an objective judgement about anything at all. Without judgements (this is better than that), it becomes impossible to make a decision. Without making decisions, it becomes impossible to run a business (or even to stay alive really). Would you ask the Dalai Lama to run your organisation?

Notes – How Not to Read This Book

- Maturana's thoughts on objectivity come from a 1985 Interview, of which I have never found the full text – only this extract. But there's much more in this vein in his many books, including *The Tree of Knowledge* [Maturana & Varela, 1987]. The idea of putting objectivity in parentheses is an altogether more philosophical (and probably more unattainable) way of achieving commitment without attachment than that proposed by Javier Bajer (see **Coach Class**, page 171).

- The review of Taleb's *The Black Swan* was by Larry Prusak, whose blog you can read at the Harvard Business Publishing website (see **Webography**).

  In the wake of the Lehman Brothers/HBOS collapse, I'm not sure whether Taleb is still a hedge fund manager. If he is, I imagine he now has to be more circumspect in announcing his profession, whose ranking has suddenly slipped to somewhere just above that of Satanic Child Abuser in the public's awareness.

- The online version of the book can be found at www.projectredstripe. blogspot.com

Lego®

A 2007 issue of the *MIT Sloan Management Review* contained an article on *Bridging Faultlines in Diverse Teams*.

Lynda Gratton and her fellow authors studied 55 project teams (as opposed to the one that I observed) and were able to reach some 'important conclusions'. Amongst these was the observation that the first faultlines that occur in teams are superficial ones that reflect surface-level attributes like gender, nationality and functional background. Later on, deeper faultlines emerge, reflecting personal values, dispositions and attitudes.

The trick, the authors further conclude, is for the team leader first to assume a task orientation (getting the team to do things), switching later on to a relationship orientation, focusing on building trust and a common culture of shared values.

In the mucky real world, which I observed, Mike Seery did a bit of both and often at the same time. Inevitably, there was more 'team-building' at the outset, when the team didn't really have anything proper to do and more 'fire-fighting' at later stages when the team had too much to do and not enough time to stop and try and fix the culture.

In the first week of the project, Mike got them to play the 'Lego game', where a Lego model was located in one room and the team had to replicate it with a supply of Lego bricks in another room. Team members were only allowed into the lavatory – where the master model resided – one at a time. They duly emerged, memorising some piece of the model, and tried to replicate it.

Though it started promisingly, problems soon emerged as team members began to move bricks that others had placed with certainty but, apparently, without precision. A strategy emerged as a result: each team member would be responsible for one area of the model, or for one colour of brick. This too dissolved in confusion.

Eventually, Mike told them that there was a saboteur in the group, who 'might be hampering the others.'

Both Stewart and Joanna were quickly and separately suspected of being the culprit and Joanna didn't touch another block after Ludwig accused her of stealing the red bricks.

Groucho Marx-like, Stewart said that he didn't trust anyone who *wanted* to play the game – a tactic which could have led to a stand-off, but didn't because enough people still wanted to get a result. Techniques were discussed for identifying the saboteur once it was realised what was happening: one member of the team was changing the master model when they went into the lavatory. But none of these techniques was properly implemented.

It was perfectly clear to me that Ludwig was the culprit. Not only was he German, but he looked guilty, answered accusations made against him defensively and uncomfortably, and gave every impression of being unhappy with his role of disrupting the group. At the end, four of the five (Mike was running the exercise rather than participating) identified Ludwig as the saboteur. Only Ludwig rightly identified Steven as the saboteur.

At the end of the day Mike asked, 'What were our takeaways from the Lego game?'.

> **Joanna:** 'I like to determine a process but everyone else seemed happy to just put their heads down and plough on. I just think the process is so critical.'
>
> **Tom:** 'Don't trust a Chinese guy.'
>
> **Mike:** 'No, it was don't rush in.'

So what was happening here? Well, for a start Mike was clearly putting himself outside the team by running the exercise rather than participating. Of course, he had to take that role if he was to introduce and run the game. The only alternative would have been to get an external facilitator to come in and run a game that Mike didn't know. (Mike later told me, 'I really did want to use someone else', and that cost was the principal reason for not using an external facilitator on occasions like this – a facilitator's daily rate would have quickly eaten into the project budget). In any case, the Lego exercise offered confirmation of how things were and would be. Mike was essentially running the show. This position had its pros and cons, which I talk about in **Leadership,** but the exercise could be seen in several ways:

- It alerted the team to problems of planning and co-ordination on an unimportant exercise and before those issues arose in a more significant context.

- It was potentially humiliating or embarrassing for the participants – and the embarrassment was observed, rather than shared, by the team leader.

- It confirmed that there was a clear hierarchy in operation.

Soon after the day of the Lego exercise, the team decided to try a different system: if one of them stood up, it was understood that they were acting as team leader until they sat down again. I never saw anyone do this but I took the idea home and agreed something similar with a colleague. In conversation, if one of us picked up a sheet of paper, we would be allowed by the other to carry on talking until we put the piece of paper down. Unsurprisingly, both experiments soon lapsed and the status quo reasserted itself – Mike led and my sentences remained unfinished. For me there was never a sense that anyone other than Mike could be the team leader; rather, from time to time, the others would challenge Mike's assumption of the role by becoming temporarily assertive or recalcitrant in their resistance to hierarchy.

Steven's conclusion in the Red Stripe public blog was as follows:

> With or without a saboteur, we made a total mess of this exercise. We did not make a plan. We did not deal with adversity. We did not work as a team. We realised afterwards that one person could have recreated the model accurately within the time period given without any help from the others. Needless to say... we need to do better when we tackle the real model.

I have reservations about games and exercises like this. They can 'fix' our assumptions too early on. The Lego game certainly was referred to later and became a significant moment in the team's own history and in the stories that it told about itself. But I think it might be useful to give a team the chance to redeem itself after an episode like this, rather than risking that it define itself as 'crap at planning'.

And this habit that we have of defining and pigeon-holing ourselves, others and our relationships with them is nowhere more clearly seen than in a team like this. As I've said, later on in the project it felt like there was never time for exercises like this. But it might have been productive to run something like it later on to shake up the team's perceptions of each other, to loosen fixed ideas and to 'promote opportunities for change'.

Still, this is nit-picking. The team looked under some quite distasteful stones during the course of the exercise and carefully examined what they found.

Dilemmas

- When you're forming a team, if you devise and run the team-building exercises yourself, you will tend to set yourself apart from the others in the group. But bringing in a facilitator or consultant to do it is expensive, time-consuming and likely to be less well focused on the particular needs of the team.

- If you run team-building exercises that highlight communication or other issues, you get early warning of potential problems but may encourage the team to develop a fixed view of itself.

- The moments in a team's trajectory when you most need to run exercises like this are, almost by definition, the moments when you haven't got time to run them.

Notes – Lego®

- The *Sloan Management Review* article is (Grattan, et al., 2007).
- The Red Stripe blog is at http://projectredstripe.com/blog/ – and the online version of this book (at www.projectredstripe.blogspot.com) links directly to the relevant sections.
- From an answer about Lego on answers.com I discover that the Danish language is a likely source for the following English words:

  Skulk ~ scoff ~ ballast ~ dangle ~ troll ~ walrus ~ iceberg ~ aquavit
  (It could be a Ted Hughes poem) ...and for the following scientific designations:

  Jacobson's organ ~ Gram's stain ~ the Bohr effect.

  Definitely my kind of language.

Ramming Speed

Tom: **'Six may be too many for a creativity team. There are too many constituencies. There aren't many bands which have got six songwriters trying to write the same song.'**

This is going to be a noisy business, I thought, when I was invited to write this book. 'Ships at a distance have every man's wish on board', as Zora Neale Hurston put it. And Project Red Stripe was certainly a wish-laden ship; one laden to the gunwales with the hopes and dreams of its participants, with the envious, spiteful or generous watchings of its onlookers, and with the cautious optimism of its Economist Group benefactors.

There was already a buzz in October 2006. A web search for Project Red Stripe led me to this:

> *Economist's New Digital Incubation Unit, Project Red Stripe*
>
> *A rather intriguing new digital incubation unit has been formed by The Economist Group, headed by Mike Seery, the CIO of The Economist Group. The new unit/project is called Project Red Stripe, and is based out of London. The mandate is to bring a new product to market… For now the group is bringing together a bunch of Economist employees to work on this full time, from the ideation phase through completion and launch.*
>
> *This unit… is completely independent, though funded by the parent company. Depending upon the kind of product it comes up with, it could wind up being spun off by the parent as a new company.*

Interesting coverage, this. First, it was a reminder that no-one at *The Economist* was trying to keep the project secret. And, second, the blog was that of journalist Rafat Ali (interviewed for *Wired* Magazine in 2003 and editor of a site that won the European Online Journalism Award in the same year and is now the foremost web-based source of information on digital content and digital media).

I doubt that Rafat had learnt about Red Stripe entirely through his own investigative efforts. If the project team were as punctilious with their project development as with their PR, I thought, they should do well.

And, of course, there's this book. In a wired age more than ever, it matters how things are seen. <u>And</u> who sees them. It was clear that *The Economist* (or the project team, at least) was not only going for 'transparency' on this project, but also for a high profile.

High profile means high risk. Whatever happened to Project Red Stripe was going to happen very much in the public eye. Project team members would each be writing their own public blog during the course of the project. As well as deciding to solicit ideas from the world at large, they would publicly describe what was happening in the team.

Ludwig would even ask the others at one point, 'Do we put the steps of the [idea-gathering] process onto the public blog and have people comment on it?' Which would have meant inviting the world-out-there to comment on how the team was going to ask the world-out-there for their ideas. I was reminded of *Knots*. Clearly, being in the public eye was part of the excitement.

In fact, project team hopefuls had been writing blogs and creating their own websites since Red Stripe was announced. One aspiring team member had created www.pickmemike.com (designed to get project leader Mike Seery to pick him, obviously enough). The Homepage announced:

> *Project Red Stripe Needs Me*
> *Because My Ideas Are Great*

And Tom Shelley's blog had been talking about Red Stripe since 20th September. By 16th October he was saying stuff like this:

> **What speed for Project Redstripe? Ramming speed.**
>
> *That is the speed that I would like to see on Project Red Stripe. We'll have the honour of working on the coolest project in the*

world. It's our duty to the history of The Economist to give it everything.

I want to order pizza in when we're working late on something that absolutely has to get done. I want to hook up at weekends to work through unexpected bugs. I want to do the web startup thing until, when we finish, everything I've got will be in that bloody project.

(Tom's use of the word duty connects with only a little contrivance to Fichte's observation about duty – discussed in **Equifinality** on page 79).

Tom's blog got me thinking about people's perceptions of this thing. It was turning into a performance. Let's do it like they do it in the movies. The late-night pizzas in particular put me in mind of *The West Wing*, (though Mike reminds me that pizzas are the staple diet on techie projects and the now infamous Robert Scoble has a picture of a few manly men 'developing and deploying late at night' and eating pizza at Microsoft). I didn't know what Tom's particular frame of reference was, but I guessed Hollywood was in there somewhere. Late night meetings where the future of the world is decided by people who are way too busy to have relationships, or cook. Tom, at least, seemed to me to be building this thing up until it was as big and exciting as anything he'd ever dreamt of. And nothing wrong with that. Talking it up would certainly get the creative energy flowing.

Back to his blog: who knows what ramming speed is? OK, Google tells me it's computer games with Viking longboats and projectiles that go at five times the speed of sound. Google also tells me that in Army of Darkness, the little Ashes yell 'ramming speed' before stabbing Ash with the fork. Mike thinks it comes from The Blues Brothers, but I can't find it – only a 1996 film called Ramming Speed, whose plot is given 10 stars and the following description by amateur critic rodeojimbo: 'Some crazy crank dealers in Texas go berzerk and kidnap a dorky schmuck for fun.' Now a dork is, apocryphally, a whale's penis, but let's not go there. Ramming speed is clearly fast. 'What speed for Project Red Stripe? Jolly fast' wouldn't have been so good.

Then, some time over Christmas I read this on Tom's blog:

Yes! I got on Project Redstripe

Yes! Yes! Yes! Yes! I'm on the team. I got it. I did it. Mouth, sing it to the sky: 'I'm doing the coolest job in the world'.

If I were Alan Shearer I'd be peeling away to the Milburn Stand with my right hand in the air. And, if I were a bell, I'd be ringing.

Tell you the truth, I've known for a while, but was told to keep schtum. I got the info just before I went to New York a month ago as I was walking to meet some friends. Whilst waiting in the cheese shop/cafe, over a lovely bottle of red and a plate of cheese, I downloaded my thoughts to the Moleskine.

... The Economist really is a publication apart. A collective of journalists dedicated to making the world understandable. Being above the rush of events, looking under appearances. Irreverent, exacting and oh so lucid.

To have this behind Project Red Stripe and to be standing on the cusp of a communication revolution brings on the shakes. We're 15 years into the Internet but the fun is only just beginning.

Oh, oh, oh my!

I'm torn between recording this moment, eating a delicious platter of cheese and ringing everyone to tell them the news.

There's an unashamed joy here. And an unashamed admiration for *The Economist*. In my day (that's, say, 25 years ago), we'd have been very, very reticent (at least in England) about splashing our dressing like this, either publicly or in private, especially about our employer. It would very definitely not have been cool.

In July, near the end of the project, Tom would say to me, 'There'll be times when I get excited about things and it gets discounted by the others because I get excited by a lot of things. Because everyone knows the next thing'll be along in a minute.'

On the other hand, Mike would say to me, 'When you talk to other people about [the project], that's when you feel good. You feel more fired up and energised. Tom's good at that. He gets that anyway.'

On 15th January, Mike announced the team members on the Red Stripe website:

- Steven Chiu
- Stewart Robinson
- Mike Seery
- Tom Shelley
- Ludwig Siegele
- Joanna Slykerman

Nothing more than that. Just their names. He had already told me a little about his intentions at our first meeting. He was looking for someone from Editorial for 'gravitas' and someone from Sales, because 'they understand the market and how to reach it', and someone who really understands the technology 'to handle the third party provider' (Mike was clear that they would be using outside experts actually to build whatever website/Internet idea they settled on, and make it happen.) But the names weren't certain then. Now they were and so I went searching:

We've met Tom Shelley via his blog. He describes himself as an 'Economist sales stooge'. He was going to find Red Stripe a lot more exciting than his regular job. He had his first gig as a stand-up comedian in July 2007. If you see his name in *Time Out*, go and listen to him.

Steven was Senior Business Development Manager for The Economist Group in Beijing. 'I was a sales guy,' he said. Mike had told me about a 'project-team possible' in Beijing. He said there might be problems because of his existing work commitments. In theory, he said, no-one at *The Economist* could stop anyone else being part of the team. But, in practice, he agreed that he might need to make some concessions. He didn't want to make too many enemies. He also said he was looking for people who wanted to go back to their jobs after the project – not for people who were trying to escape them or looking for a six-month holiday. (When the team met, its members were interested to discover that five out six of them intended <u>not</u> to go back to their original role, after all.)

There was almost nothing about Steven on the Web. Later I learnt that he is from Newfoundland, where they don't need to make artificial fog. When I asked him in the sixth month what he would do differently, were he to do a Project Red Stripe again, he answered immediately, 'I wouldn't do it again; it would be too hard for the family.' (Punctuating other people's speech is interesting. I think he spoke the semicolon, but I can't be sure.)

Stewart was a technologically skilled operator. He's credited with others for web development work for *The Economist*'s 'The World in 2004' and was on the development team that built and ran CFO.com and Economist.com.

Here's what he said at the outset on his blog:

Tuesday, January 02, 2007

Secondment

Maturing The Economist Group's web IT infrastructure will have to wait for me at least.

I've been accepted to an elite super group of corporate paratroopers. We will be incubating our very own digital divide skipping child. It will have 6 parents. Arnie and Danny had 7, I think, in Twins (the movie).

We will be planting seeds for The Economist's newest venture. M&A's aren't easy money so every so often I guess you have to try doing something yourself. I wonder whether our competitor to myspace/youtube/google/breathing/talking/ communicating will work. Why am I picturing the baby from Charmed who scares off dates for Mommy with a white light in his mouth?

I have to say my application to join was terrible, really terrible. I wrote about software instead of innovation. It's because I'm crap, and a little because I was in the middle of the JoelOnSoftware book. However I did muck about and make my blog inaccessible and break the up and down arrow keys in the process. The css is nice, the first time you load it and you get your posts in a viewport. I basically think I got in because I lent a playstation 2 eyetoy to Mike Seery for the web cast. Mum, I told you gaming would get me somewhere.

Forget the application however, the interview was a joke. I interview a few people in my existing role. I sat with Mike in a Pret and proceeded to answer 'Yes I can do that' and 'That won't be a problem' without any justification. To be fair to me a little bit, as I already work for Mike albeit through the onion of management I didn't realise I would be interviewed in such a real way. It clearly must be the eyetoy, or perhaps it was the eyetoy drivers that make it work so well on a pc.

I join a cast of superstars from The Economist.

The online version links to Stew's application – but here's an excerpt:

Dear Mike,

I'd like to join Redstripe for so many reasons. I'd like to be part of something completely new and web based. I love the idea of 'doing it for the kids' erm perhaps. I read so much lately about how to make software correctly and we can't quite get that right in Digital Media just now but we are making tracks. I am a complete web geek and although I think web2.0 is a marketing pile of rubbish. I love social software, the very idea of it... I think I can offer creativity, honest hard graft and the best hands on technical skills you are likely to get in the group at least until Mick joins next week. Techies who can actually communicate with non-techies are rare and should be cherished. I believe I'm one of these people. I'm slightly disappointed to be honest with my application. It's a lame blog partly hidden with some flashy javascript as you'll see.

I care about getting things right. I want to build something brand new. I want to be a part of this because I think we can make something that could possibly make the newspaper second in value to the group. And you know what, if we fail, I'd like the practices we use in building the product and I don't just mean technically, to be brought back into the group as lessons we can learn. I can't see any possibility of failure on the investment from the group's point of view if we figure out better methods for running businesses. Although I'm sure they'll have a different opinion.

Pick me, we'll win.

Stew

Ludwig Siegele 'started his journalistic career in 1990 as the Paris Business and Political Correspondent of *Die Zeit*. In 1995, he moved from France to California to write about the Internet revolution, first for *Die Zeit* and then for *The Economist*. In 1998 he became the US Technology Correspondent for *The Economist*, based near Silicon Valley. In 2003 Ludwig moved to Berlin as Germany correspondent.' That's all I could find out about him at the start. I know precious little more now. Except that I would trust completely his articles in *The Economist*, if I only knew which ones he had written.

Google found me nothing whatsoever on Joanna. Even today it doesn't find me much. As the Economist Intelligence Unit's EMEA Marketing Manager she kept an enviably low profile. (This, of course, raises questions about the whole business of 'personal branding' and highlights one of the less discussed implications of changing your name when you marry – that you lose your Google profile overnight.) No surprise, then, that she subsequently contributed to the Red Stripe blog as follows:

Exposing one's soul is not something I would naturally choose to do, let alone in public. To share my deepest thoughts and concerns is a practice I would usually reserve for a select and intimate few. Yet the web in its current incarnation seems to challenge this notion head on.

Through blogs and social forums, not only does one expose oneself to an unknown audience. This exposure also invites both Judgement and interaction. I am not comfortable with this exposure. As a result, I find blogging difficult.

I like to be able to define my audience and to manage both the output and likely level of interaction. It takes a newly sought boldness to relax these requirements, to just write and be open to whatever the web will offer up in response, if anything....

I approach this world with hesitation [the world of blogging and the web]. I see that perhaps the potential costs to pride, control and privacy may be worth the possible benefits.

Google "I approach this world with hesitation" and – though it may change – you'll find that hers is the only voice saying those words. If, like me, you become enthusiastic about this line of research, try Googling "I approach the world with..." and see what it comes up with. Here's what I found the other day:

- little fear, no corduroy clothing, clean underwear and a lot of self belief
- an 'open book' mentality
- a more positive outlook
- [no] negative lilt
- a very 'problem-solving' approach
- curiosity (x3)
- an open heart
- a new wariness
- the eyes of an artist, the ears of a musician and the soul of a writer
- an open mind (x2)
- my moral judgement and values
- confidence
- a sense of wonder, curiosity, adventure, humor, discovery and playfulness

- ideological blinders
- a set of Sicilian rules and values
- a certain fashion of hope and belief
- a new feminist perspective
- trembling arms [and] a humming in my head
- a distinct sense of harmony
- a blindfold and a smile
- a scientific bent

Mike Seery I'd met just before the project started. But it was from the team blog that I learnt that he was a computer man through and through (though not only that, of course). He'd started his working life at the Cabinet Office and worked his way up/down to becoming Chief Information Officer at *The Economist* after a long stint with the group. He also revealed that his passions include his family and a football team called Arsenal and that his favourite innovations were the domestic smoke alarm, the Waterfield Designs Cargo Bag and the iPod.

I'd asked Mike whether he was planning to do psychometric profiling as part of the process of choosing team members. He wasn't, but he probably would once the team was formed, as part of the team building process. He's well respected and well established, but he still hadn't ever run a project like this before. It mattered to him. It was his idea and he'd had to do some politics to get the idea off the ground. I asked if he'd had to make compromises with The Economist Group's management team. He'd had to agree to report back to Helen Alexander, the CEO, every two weeks, when he'd wanted to wait until the project was complete before making any kind of report. But he'd managed to persuade her that the project team should not have to present a series of draft ideas, with the GMC giving the green light to one of them. Independence was important. Autonomy.

For First World economists and sociologists, 'autonomy' is a highly-prized state; a key indicator that things are moving in the right direction. In Anglo-Saxon psychotherapy, 'autonomy' is one of the key definers of the appropriately developed adult ego. In the West, we like autonomy.

I wonder if it's an over-rated virtue. How about the ability to understand one's place in the world, in the warp and weft of relationship, without exaggerating it or understating it? (One word for that ability to maintain an appropriate sense of proportion is 'humility'.)

Dilemmas

- Blogging, or otherwise being very public, about an innovation project, has many advantages. Not least of these is that raising the public profile generates excitement and enthusiasm. But it can also sink into navel-gazing and blogging about the blog.

- Recruiting team members who want to return to their old jobs at the end of the project helps ensure that you don't just hire the disaffected. But the disaffected may also be the most creative.

- Building the excitement about a project like this obviously helps ensure enthusiastic commitment from the team. But, if it becomes 'the best job in the world', there may also be a need to come up with 'the best idea in the world'. Which takes us back to Moby-Dick.

- How can an organisation promote a sense of appropriate proportion and humility without sounding like a damp Christian Union student in a blue anorak?

- In the same vein, and as with child rearing, how do you find a proper balance between adventuring and hesitating?

Notes – Ramming Speed

- The 'ships quote' is the first line of (Hurston, 1937).
- The extract entitled **Economist's New Digital Incubation Unit, Project Red Stripe** is from www.paidcontent.org, a website which sets out to offer international coverage of new media issues and the business of managing digital content.
- *Knots* is (Laing, 1970).
- Tom Shelley's blog (Fedoral Reserve) is listed in the **Blography**.
- In January 2008, Microsoft's Robert Scoble (author of the scobleizer blog) had his Facebook account disabled because he ran an automated script to scrape his friends' contact details and export them to Plaxo. (If you find this note as patronising as one explaining that a bicycle has two wheels, please bear in mind that some readers will find no part of the previous sentence meaningful.)
- Stewart's blog (Stewsnooze) is listed in the **Blography**.
- *The Economist* doesn't use bylines.

Drifting, Angst and Pan-ic

Joanna: *'I feel a little bit paralysed at the moment.'*

One of the many tensions (and I mean tension in a Newton's 3rd Law kind of way) apparent in Project Red Stripe related to direction-finding, goals, intentions and wandering around.

With its very broad remit, Project Red Stripe gave its members enormous scope for 'wandering about' and looking for, or waiting for, inspiration. Now, of course, this is in the very nature of an innovation team and one of the primary characteristics that distinguishes it from a more goal-oriented project team. Yet this innovation team also had a very clear sense of having a goal: 'creating an innovative and web-based product, service or business model by July 2007'. It just didn't yet know what the goal looked like. Its task was to locate the goal and then get there.

This set up tensions from the outset. There was a strong feeling at different times that the team was wasting time. Against this was the clear sense that the team ought to take its time in identifying the right idea – because there was surely no point in spending six months writing business and marketing plans, developing websites and other infrastructure, working with partners and commercialising the idea, if they hadn't chosen the right one in the first place.

This often reminded me of 'drifting'. Drifting has been developed as a performance art, as autobiogeography, as a philosophical study and as a literary style (as well as a way of exploring the urban landscape). Its masters and mistresses (if you can master and mistress something as elusive as drifting) are the Wrights and Sites team.

It seems to me that drifting has particular relevance to the innovation project team where it pays attention to the idea of determination. Baz Kershaw, formerly Professor of Drama at Bristol University, although he's not a drifter as far as I know, has talked about the way in which our experience at a zoo is 'over-determined': signs, paths, maps and guides structure the route we walk; information notices structure the way we look at and experience the creatures; cages, enclosures and access points structure the way we observe and what we observe – and all this in addition to the particular memories and experiences we may bring, the cultural associations and responses that we may carry with us, and so on. Cities have a similar effect: there are explicit and implicit rules about where we can go and where we can't; where we can stop, stand and sit and where we must walk; what we can look at and what we can't; even how fast we should walk or on what side of the pavement.

All of this 'over-determination' in the city or in the zoo makes it hard to 'just drift'.

Some of these same rules come into play in an innovation project. The team members have their own expectations and associations, have their own experience of groups, reactions to rules and authority, working preferences and so on. They will also tend, such being our habit in this country and at this time, to look for some rules and guidelines, to establish where the power and the authority lies, to set down – if there aren't any already in place – codes of conduct, attendance times and working policies.

Inevitably, this sought-after regimentation can be at odds with the 'right to roam', which is the passport of the innovative and inventive mind. Just as drifting largely dispenses with maps and destinations and attempts to journey without intention (what Walter Benjamin has called 'the rhythmics of... slumber'), so we can suppose that innovation might attempt to dispense with as many limiting conventions as possible, in order to facilitate the emergence of ideas. Though creating a regime within which regimentation is discouraged is itself paradoxical.

One of the by-products of drifting or, more specifically, of the absence of rules, form and shape that accompany it, is a sense of panic. There is a hegemony of rules and shapes and laws precisely because we feel chillingly uncomfortable without them. Phil Smith has described this kind of panic as an '*encounter with everything (else), an intense, but relatively common initiatory Pan-ic – an experience of causeless, but sited dread*' – the hyphenation of pan-ic reminds us of the word's Greek origins and associations with the god Pan and the word 'pan' meaning everything in a pantechnicon sort of way.

In this form, panic is closely related to Kierkegaard's existential angst or dread. This dread is explicitly connected with freedom and choices, with the uncertainties and unboundariedness that freedom entails: 'the dread felt by innocence, which is the reflex of freedom within itself at the thought of its possibility.'

That may sound ridiculously grand. I'm sure none of the members of the team felt they were experiencing existential angst. But there was a sense of panic at times, when the team realised that they could do *anything*, but that they only had six months to do it. And I also connect that panic with their need to find the 'big idea', the becoming-whale-of-an-idea.

So, the Red Stripe team sometimes wandered around without a clear sense of what was going to happen next and without clear rules about how it might be going to happen or what they should be doing about it. Jurgen Habermas talks about something like this when he discusses 'action oriented to success' and 'action oriented to understanding' and the different modes of thinking and communication that they require (logical and pragmatic for the first; rhizomatic and affective for the second).

Movement artist Sandra Reeve says much the same when discussing action preceding intention:

> In **Move into Life** practice, I often start from movement tasks or moving with no fixed intention in a natural environment and allow associations, feelings, images and ultimately meaning to emerge from a constantly shifting context. Sometimes I introduce a theme, in order to guide the direction of my creative response... This corresponds with Gibson's theory of affordances: that is, how we pick up information appropriate to our needs directly from the environment.

In any case, the team was 'drifting'. Instinctively, that seems like an appropriate thing for an innovation team to do; but it's also an uncomfortable thing to do at any time, and especially in a business context.

For myself, I would choose this state of drifting as the most profoundly productive one. Others would say that safety is a prerequisite of productive enquiry or creativity. Arie de Geus maintains that 'fear inhibits learning'. Probably all these views are correct. Certainly there are many, including some members of the Red Stripe team, who work hardest and fastest when they know where they're going. Perhaps it depends on the make-up of your team, or perhaps your team can be invited to approach panic and safety in a new light. In any case, we could say that the issue of drifting and panic and over-determination needs to be addressed explicitly, at least if safety is intended.

[Incidentally, I like these words of Borges: *la inminencia de una revelación, que no se produce* (the imminence of a revelation that does not take place). They seem to me to characterise much of the early part of Project Red Stripe's existence and, perhaps, that of many other such innovation projects].

Just before we leave the question of wandering around:

Tim Ingold, writing about String Bags and Birds' Nests, suggests that we might look at construction as a kind of weaving, rather than as a kind of making:

> *Whereas making defines an activity in terms of its capacity to yield a finished object, weaving focuses on the skilled character of the process by which that object comes into existence. Three important properties of technical skill are highlighted. First, skill is not a property of the individual human body in isolation but of the whole system of relations constituted by the presence of the artisan in a richly structured environment. Secondly, rather than representing the mere mechanical application of external force, skill involves qualities of care, judgement and dexterity.*

Thirdly, skilled action has a narrative quality, in the sense that every movement grows rhythmically out of the one before and lays the groundwork for the next.

Perhaps innovation, as well as construction, can be looked at as a kind of weaving.

Dilemmas

- Drifting 'aimlessly' can be a profoundly creative process, but it's also anxiety-inducing. Participants (and Finance Directors) may want something more regimented. Rules and guidelines can offer direction or serve as blinkers.

- It's vitally important to ensure that you've picked the right idea before embarking on commercialising it. But equally important to know when to stop looking for the right idea and accept that the one you have is good enough.

- As Oliver Burkeman says, 'attempts to induce good feelings through top-down effort are self-defeating – whether imposed on workers by management or imposed on yourself by your rational brain... you (or those you manage) get caught in the psychological trap known as the double bind – the unspoken demand whereby, in the words of the philosopher Alan Watts, "you are required to do something that will be acceptable only if you do it voluntarily"'. Just how do you direct people to do the right thing?

- Hip organisations (Andrew Jones lists a lot of them) often set out to create a regime within which regimentation is discouraged. That's also precisely what some innovation projects set out to do. It's anomalous.

- Action oriented to understanding should probably precede action oriented to success, but who decides how and when to change emphasis from one to the other?

Notes – Drifting, Angst and Pan-ic

- The Wright & Sites website is in the **Webography** and there's much more on all this in *Dread, Route and Time*, see [Smith, 2003].

- [Jenks, 1995] is a good introduction to drifting and the flâneur and the Wrights & Sites website (above) has an excellent Links section.

- On over-determination, I paraphrase from a paper called 'Becoming in Between: Zoological Performance for the Ecological Era', given by Professor Kershaw at Bristol University in Summer 2006.

- Walter Benjamin is quoted in [Hodge, 2006, p.49].

- For more from Phil Smith see [Smith, 2003].

- If you have an appetite for angst, see [Kierkegaard, 1957, p.50].

- Habermas [1961] doesn't use the term rhizomatic, as far as I know. That's my interpolation. But he does discuss at length Weber's 'iron cage of modernity', which he sees as emerging from a Lebenswelt dominated by rationalisation and hierarchy/domination. For Habermas, salvation lies in the incorporation of alternative, non-rational approaches to communication and change and through resistance to the rationalist imperative. This resistance he saw embodied in movements like feminism and environmentalism. (This latter point relates to the issues raised in **Profitability and Systems Thinking**, page 89, and the difficult question of how to balance commercial and ethical values and imperatives in the development of a business.)

- See [Reeve, 2008] for more on the fascinating question of action preceding perception, understanding and meaning – a process studied most particularly by Jaak Panksepp [2006].

- Arie de Geus talks at some length about fear and learning in *The Living Company* [de Geus, 1999, p.143].

- The quotes towards the end of the chapter are from, respectively, [Borges, 1964], [Ingold, 2000] and [Burkeman, 2008].

- Andrew Jones analyses a number of 'human-centred enterprises' that focus on design, architecture and anthropology in [Jones, 2008].

Maps

Mike: **'Let's put a huge Google Maps marker flag on top of The Economist building so it appears on Google Earth.'**

At the end of their first week, Mike asked each member of the team to produce a map of where they had been so far and to 'sell' their map to the rest of the team.

Three of the maps were 'geographic', in that they plotted where the team had been physically (they had been on a couple of 'team-building' trips in London and had been to Regent's Park to have a meeting where they shared their own 'big ideas' for Project Red Stripe. Stewart had used Google Maps to record where they had been on their trips, while Steven used Google Earth to show his journey from Beijing, his natal Canada and the team's current digs. Both were technically excellent and applauded by the rest of the team. Mike, who was the only one to remember his own instruction to 'sell' the map to the others, produced a map on tracing paper, which could be overlaid onto an atlas, given to others as a walking tour of London or resized on a photocopier.

It became clear from Mike's comments that he had intended them to produce a physical map of where they had been, rather than something that would only qualify as a map in a fairly loosely metaphorical world. This immediately raised some anxieties among the others about whether they had done the exercise wrong and this, on and off, was to be an anxiety that recurred for some members of the group. Perhaps there's a lesson here for innovation teams, where the notion of getting it right is even harder to pin down than it is for most teams. It's a cliché in business that it's only by making mistakes and getting things wrong that you learn how to get them right. So, in a group like this, it may be really important to work out at the start in what ways team members are allowed to get things wrong. It ought, according to the theory, to be an all-embracing acceptance, but getting things wrong by not turning up or not doing any work or consistently failing to meet self-imposed targets might be too much for any team to bear.

[An enchanting possibility emerges from recent brain research:

> 'we can predict the likelihood of someone making an error
> about six seconds in advance, with gradual changes starting as
> much as 30 seconds ahead of time'.

The research is reported in *The Economist* and the article goes on
to suggest that people could wear hats that would alert others
to the likelihood of them making a mistake. Clearly this relates
only to certain types of task, at this stage, but the principle of
detecting changing attention patterns could apply more broadly.
Imagine the mounting pressure on a chess grandmaster or World
Cup penalty-taker or business decision-maker or woman trying to
decide whether to dump her bloke. Would the flashing hat (alerting
themselves and others to the impending error) help prevent the
error or increase stress levels to a point where a different error was
more likely?]

On with the maps. Ludwig used a piece of visual content
management software called 'TheBrain' to represent the areas
that the project team had been working on rather than the
geographic places they had visited. He was on something of a
mission, announcing in his soft mid-Atlantic accent (which can
make it hard to tell that he's German until a word with a leading
'w' looms into view) that 'I no longer want to be the scribe, but if
you want me to be the master of TheBrain, I can do that'. The team
never took him up on his offer and he continued to do most of the
formal writing for the team, although he largely didn't record their
discussions any longer. In spite of his suggestion that the team used
TheBrain to save and display information, they opted to use 'Central
Desktop'. With its very traditional, hierarchical, information-storage
structure, Central Desktop was probably not the most creatively
useful software tool for them, though it made finding stuff easy.
How much time should you devote at the outset to getting the
technology right?

Joanna (the only Feeler in a team with five other Thinkers according
to their recent Myers-Briggs initiation: game and first set to Myers-
Briggs) mapped, amongst other things, her feelings – which

included hesitation, trepidation and excitement, though Gerard Fairtlough later told me that she seemed to him 'to be the person who was the strongest'. Her map was on a single sheet of A4 and showed a series of loops (sharing ideas, getting to know each other, etc.) which all turned back on themselves and on each other. She said that the first week had 'felt like you were planning your big overseas trip; you'd been out and bought your backpack, done your research, and so on'. It was the only thing I ever heard her say that betrayed her Australian origins, though her accent and High Rising Terminal did so constantly, of course. She judged that the team was preparing itself before moving. She named 'severe doubt' and 'fear' amongst her feelings during the week – feelings that, in another context, might have been more fully addressed by the others. Here they were heard and the next map presentation began.

Tom (observing that 'we have been places emotionally as well as physically') had all sorts of stuff going on including Paradiso on coat hangers on the spiral staircase and Inferno under the desks. You had to crawl under the desks and lie on the trailing sockets to read the contents of Inferno. Here were to be found:

- Failure
- No fun
- Hell
- Judging
- No hope
- Jealousy
- Blame
- Undeliverables
- Bitterness
- Disloyalty

Gerard Egan and Bill Tate have both written about managing and auditing the shadow side of the organisation – but few others have paid it much attention. (Although, of course, it lurks under every stone in conversations about corporate governance, business ethics and the like.) And here it was, being manifested before my eyes.

I think that every work group, project or process team, department or small business should have its own version of Inferno posted somewhere significant – just to remind themselves of the things they don't get to talk about. The contents should be as specific as possible – not just greed or ambition or lust, but clear examples of these shadowy 'behaviours' in action.

Dilemmas

- Giving permission for team members to get things wrong is the new mantra. But it may not be as simple as it seems. Obviously, there are times when you absolutely need them *not* to get things wrong. And some mistakes are much more fruitful than others. It's probably helpful to come up with clear guidelines rather than a blanket permission, but there's always a trade-off between control and opportunity.

- Like teambuilding, or any other form of preparation, time spent getting the right systems and technology in place is – on the face of it – always time well spent. But things change. What if you use mind-mapping software that people don't know well or find poorly suited to their needs? What if you adopt a more familiar and easy-to-use file management system but subsequently find that it unduly constrains information-sharing?

- Paying attention early on to the 'shadow side' looks like the perfect solution to unspoken fears, tensions and rivalries. If you don't do it, you risk never addressing those issues. Do it, and you risk unsettling team members or replacing one set of unrealistic 'hope beliefs' with another set of 'failure fears'.

Notes – Maps

- There's more about the Regent's Park meeting in **Those Ideas in Full** (page 208).
- The research on anticipating errors is reported in [Economist, 2008].
- Details of TheBrain and Central Desktop are to be found in the **Webography**.
- There's more on the Myers-Briggs findings in **Stages of the Group** (page 50).
- The books on the organisation shadow side are [Egan, 1994] and [Tate, 2003].

Creativity and Innovation

Joanna: *'There's this idea that you can only create great ideas in a free-form, unstructured environment. I don't believe that.'*

In *Creativity is not Enough*, Professor Ted Levitt (who later became editor of the *Harvard Business Review* and popularised the term 'globalisation') said interesting things about creativity and innovation:

> It is alleged that everything in American business would be just dandy if industry were simply more creative and if it would hire more creative people and give them the chance to show their fructifying stuff.

It seems to me that the world would be a better place if more Harvard Professors used terms like 'fructifying stuff' and my fantasy is that, of the two terms, he'd rather be famous for that than globalisation.

Levitt goes on to explain his view that:

> ... there is really very little shortage of creativity and of creative people in American business. The major problem is that so-called creative people often (though certainly not always) pass off on others the responsibility for getting down to brass tacks. They have plenty of ideas but little businesslike follow-through. They do not make the right kind of effort to help their ideas get a hearing and a try.

His point, clearly enough, is that ideation in businesses is relatively abundant. It is its implementation that is more scarce. Which brings us back to one of the conventional distinctions made by people who attempt to define innovation and creativity: namely that creativity is about having the idea, while innovation is about making it happen. (As it turned out, implementation was one of the particular strengths of the team, see **Open Innovation**, page 105.)

In this sense, Red Stripe had the perfect brief. It had not only to have the big idea or ideas, it had to 'pick one or more of these ideas to develop, and then bring the idea(s) to market'.

Another point made by Levitt in the same article is that 'in most business organisations, the most continually creative men... are also generally known as corporate malcontents.' For whatever reason (Mike Seery says the team members were chosen 'for their flexibility, enthusiasm and to get a range of experience within the team'), the Red Stripe team members were far from corporate malcontents. Of course, they were not all unreserved admirers of their employer but, by and large, they liked and respected *The Economist*, were proud to work for it and determined to do well by it during the six months of the project. Perhaps, if the team really had been capable, as Slashdot suggested, of frittering away the six months on drink and debauchery, then they might also have been even more receptive to even more revolutionary thinking:

> *In the first week, the staffers bought beer, wine, whisky, condoms, flat screen televisions and gaming consoles.*

> *In the second week, the staffers hired a young graphic artist through the Internet for $35 per hour to set up a rudimentary web page asking for innovative ideas.*

> *The next 5 months is a blur.*

> *The final two weeks were a flurry of activities. So many good ideas to review! So little time!*

By contrast, it was their respect for The Economist Group and concern not to do anything that might damage its reputation (or concern for their jobs, or conservatism, or pragmatism... call it what you like) that led them to back off from their brief at times. When they could have gone public with the **Lughenjo** idea and effectively forced the hand of The Economist Group (who would not have wanted to be seen ditching an admirably philanthropic scheme), they deliberately chose to stay silent and seek approval from the GMC first.

Staying with Ted Levitt, he further noted:

> *There is some evidence that the relatively rigid organisation can build into its own structure certain flexibilities which*

would provide an organisational home for the creative but irresponsible individual. What may be required, especially in the large organisation, is not so much a suggestion box scheme as a specialised group whose function is to receive ideas, work them out, and follow them through in the necessary manner.

One of the bravest decisions that Project Red Stripe took in its early days was to abandon the great ideas that most of its members had brought with them and, in some cases, which they had worked up into virtual business plans in order to get accepted onto the team. (Joanna didn't have an idea at the outset and, as a result, felt somewhat split off from those who were 'awash with them'.) After presenting their ideas to each other on a cold day in Regent's Park, the team set about finding ways to harvest ideas from *Economist* readers and other interested parties. In using this crowdsourcing approach, they defied James Surowiecki, the granddaddy of crowd stuff, who claims that 'despite compelling evidence that executives and experts are poor at making decisions, and that the collective wisdom of large numbers of people is very much better at it, few businesses rigorously canvass their employees and customers for anything more than inconsequential assessments after the decisions have already been made'.

For the first few weeks they simply concentrated on developing a workable scheme for collecting, collating, sorting, classifying and evaluating these ideas.

As a result they put themselves at a stroke in exactly the position of the 'responsible' evaluation group rather than that of the 'irresponsible' creative individual.

One reason this was such a bold decision was that it effectively undermined one of the most significant 'glues' that the team started out with – the notion that they could come up with an idea that would change the face of business, or the world, or – at the very least – *The Economist*. In looking outwards for ideas, they freed themselves temporarily from the clutch of the becoming-whale-of-an-idea.

Dilemmas

- If good ideas are relatively abundant but the ability to commercialise them is relatively scarce, it may be useful to focus on the latter. But, if you do that, you might end up missing out on the *really* good idea, which no-one has had yet.

- The crowd will come up with good ideas but it may also be tainted by lowest-common-denominator thinking.

- Sourcing ideas from outside the group can have the function of removing the creative spark from those doing the innovating.

- A less responsible (or more malcontent) bunch than the Project Red Stripe team might have pursued the idea of a philanthropy website and launched it in a blaze of publicity without approval from the GMC. The Economist Group would have got 'businesslike follow-through' but would also have got an innovation it didn't want.

Notes – Creativity and Innovation

- The fructifying quotes are from [Levitt, 1963]. I know it was a long time ago.
- Almost every book on creativity or innovation has a discussion of what these and related terms might mean, which can make for dull reading, given that they're terms that we invented to describe fairly woolly processes rather than names for tangibly different things, like an oak tree and an ash tree. If you're fascinated by the subject, a paper entitled 'Differentiating creativity, innovation, entrepreneurship, intrapreneurship, copyright and patenting of IS products/processes', published in *Proceedings of the Twenty-Third Annual Hawaii International Conference on System Sciences, 1990* should slake your appetite.
- The beer, wine and whisky extract is from slashdot.org – a website that announces itself as having 'News for Nerds. Stuff that Matters'. And it does. Incidentally, one of the benefits of subscribing to the site is that you get to read each story 10-20 minutes before it goes public, which goes some way towards explaining why no-one has time to cook any more.
- On crowdsourcing, see [Surowiecki, 2005]. The description of Surowiecki's approach is Dave Pollard's and taken from his excellent blog, *How to Save the World* (see **Biography**). I couldn't have put it better myself, so I didn't.

Dogging

Another of the team's bold, early decisions was to operate in as public a manner as possible – with a website, a blog, even a webcam to tell the world what they were up to. Of course, this very public profile was an enormous help to them in the knowledge-harvesting phase of the project, though they later effectively went underground in order to preserve some secrecy as their planning evolved.

[Dwayne Melancon has some interesting thoughts on this. Talking about the risks and advantages of going public with your idea, he says:

> Of course, there are risks in early disclosure. You may give away your secrets and your competitors may gain advantage from what you have released. In business, as with your own ideas, there are multiple ways to address this:
>
> - **Plentiful attitude.** Assume there are enough ideas, money, opportunity, etc. to go around and share the idea openly. This approach also works for ideas you are contributing for the greater good (open standards, for example).
>
> - **Scarcity attitude.** Assume that revealing your ideas early will expose you to the risk of being out-executed, or having your idea show up in others' works. You can control this to a certain degree by limiting disclosure (to a selected group of early adopters, for example), or by putting a non-disclosure agreement in place. In this case, pick your friends wisely.
>
> And there are many shades between these two. Regardless of the end of the spectrum on which you find yourself, there can be a lot of value and 'time to market' benefits of going ugly early. Consider this powerful tool in your toolbox – are you incubating any ideas that could benefit from going ugly early?]

They continued to draw on the glue and energy that the possibility of changing the world offered. In mid-May, Stewart asked the group whether they felt it was too 'cheesy' to end an email to the website design agency with the words 'Let's change the world'. Perhaps predictably, it was Tom who responded, 'Not cheesy enough'.

The early decision about idea-harvesting also had the effect of leaving Red Stripe with dozens of good, workable ideas, some of which, with the right backing, could have made money for *The Economist*. Some specific ones, not mentioned in detail in **Bright Ideas** (page 168), were:

- An elite editing tool
- *Economist* networking events online
- Intelligent product placement for advertisers
- Allowing readers to choose which perspective they want to read a story from
- Getting crisis information to key aid workers
- A Freecycle network for skills

Although Red Stripe blogged about the ideas they received, they (understandably) didn't devote any further time to them because they were concentrating on their chosen idea. Equally, these ideas were never presented to the Group Management Committee. The result is that some of the harvested ideas have effectively been left out in the field rather than brought in for the winter. Ironically, this might have been avoided if Mike had accepted Helen Alexander's idea of having the team present a range of ideas to the GMC. The GMC would then have picked their preferred idea and been aware of the other ones. Of course, the downside that Mike had rightly spotted was that they would have spent a huge amount of time working up business ideas to no avail. (As I write, it's becoming clear, however, that some of the harvested ideas <u>are</u> being incorporated into the Economist.com website.)

Back in 1960, Murray D. Lincoln, president of the Nationwide Insurance Company, advocated the notion of a company having a vice-president in charge of revolution. The Economist Group effectively got itself a committee in charge of revolution when it approved the setting up of Project Red Stripe. And with their idea-harvesting process, Red Stripe effectively bought themselves, if not the blueprints for, at least the seeds of, enough revolutions to keep the business happy for a while.

Let's take the Group's decision to set up a committee in charge of revolution, first. It's worth putting this in context. In the year to March 2008 (which includes most of the time Project Red Stripe was under way):

Economist.com had:	about 3 million unique users (up 39% on the previous year)
	199 million page views (up 30%)
The Economist Group achieved:	revenue of £266.4 million (up 8% on the previous year)
	profit of £44.3 million (up 23%).

These were good results by any standards, and especially good in the media sector. As we see in **Reading Matter** (page 134), companies are notoriously bad at fomenting revolution when things are going really well. So, supporting your CIO in withdrawing from the fray for six months to foment a revolution at a time when your website – and your business as a whole – is generating significant growth is a spectacular decision.

One of the intentions of this book is to set out for other potential corporate innovators what lessons can be learnt from *The Economist*'s path-breaking approach. One immediate riposte could be that the company was not breaking new paths at all. Isn't the business of innovation – specifically on or via the Web – exactly what countless hordes of people and organisations have been doing since about 1994? An answer is that you don't get to read about many of them at any length. But you <u>are</u> reading about *The Economist*. In part, that's because of the very public profile they chose to adopt. It's also a function of *The Economist*'s name. The activities of the Acme Manufacturing Co. would almost certainly have been of less interest to most of us. Which goes to show that celebrity is not just a function of lowest common denominator television but also a side-effect of capitalism.

Dilemmas

- If you go public too soon, you risk losing a competitive advantage. If you do it too late, you don't get the benefit of informed input from outsiders. As always, there's a trade-off.

- In an innovation team it's more important than ever to include Creator/Innovators and Concluder/Producers, but the tensions between them are likely to be greater than usual given the demands of the project.

- When things are going really well, it's often the best possible time to foment a revolution. But it can also seem like an unnecessary distraction. Most tend to wait until things are going badly – not such a good time, unless you follow the Last Fart of the Ferret school of thought (see page 117).

Notes – Dogging

- Dwayne Melancon's blog (see **Biography**) is always worth reading, though it's slightly alarming that he told us how to create an online countdown timer to remind us how many days were left to do our Christmas shopping.
- For more on the idea of a vice-president in charge of revolution, see [Karp and Lincoln, 1960].
- Creator/Innovator and Concluder/Producer are the terms preferred by Margerison and McCann for their TMS Wheel – see [Margerison, 2002] – but every psychometric profiling system has its equivalents.

Success

Tom's Inferno (described in **Maps** on page 35) reflects many of the definitions of failure that the team had identified during a group exercise in February on success and failure. The next day, the flip-chart outputs from that exercise festooned the walls of the tiny office. In the idea cloud buzzing around 'success' I saw:

> Launch ~ work as a team ~ Red Stripe 2.0 ~ 100,000 users ~ confidence ~ GMC (Group Management Committee) happy ~ make money ~ gain respect ~ healthy ~ do it in six months ~ being hired permanently by Red Stripe ~ learning ~ making something cool.

And around 'failure':

> No product ~ fighting ~ getting fired ~ leaving the team ~ GMC don't like it ~ goes bust ~ egg on face ~ boring ~ incremental ~ old business model ~ shame.

At the end of March, Javier, the team coach, asked them each what success would look like.

> **Tom:** 'Success would look like a really, really, really great website which kicked ass and set me up with doing something at *The Economist* or fun elsewhere. A kickass website.'

> **Mike:** 'getting the green light from *The Economist* to do whatever we want to do.'

> **Steven:** 'To have created something innovative, new, where peers and colleagues stood up and took notice... something that we'd get recognised for.'

> **Joanna:** 'A thing, most likely a website, that impressed internally because whilst appearing to be something seemingly simple (we only have 6 months) it was clear it had significant future potential for The Economist Group, whilst paradoxically outsiders might see it as a fairly small development, unaware of its potential.

> **Ludwig:** 'Something fun to implement where people say "wow", that gets recognition. Something that's useful to the target group and useful to The Economist Group, that guarantees Project Red Stripe is not just a one-off.'
>
> **Stewart:** 'Something I'm a serious part of.'

As always, recognition, visibility and making an impression were important for them. And why not? Why come up with an idea that nobody rated? But important to notice that one person's success is getting somewhere, another's is being recognised for it and a third's is being involved along the way.

Clearly, by their own definitions, Project Red Stripe failed. But what if the definitions were wrong in the first place? As Scott Anthony says in a thoughtful piece:

> The Economist *actually got exactly what it asked for: an innovative idea that was ready to launch quickly. Had it been clearer up front that a critical success factor was the ability to generate some kind of economic return, it is possible that the Red Stripe team would have developed a vastly different idea.*

And that's exactly right. In the weeks they spent developing first the idea known as **Bavaria** (relating to universal primary education) and then **Lughenjo** (a broader, philanthropic, not-for-profit) the team were deliberately turning away from commercial innovations. Let The Economist Group, they said, make its next reputation as a doer-of-good and the core business can only benefit. They had come up with a radical innovation in a complete departure from the company's publishing past. They had a product in their sights but moved away from it in large part because of the reaction from the Group Management Committee (GMC).

Nothing they came up with was boring or incremental. Clearly, for the team members individually, the six-month stint was an extraordinary learning opportunity, which they took every advantage of. For *The Economist* the lessons and opportunities potentially emerging from the project are huge (there's more on this in **The Practical Visionary** on page 141). As Scott Anthony goes on to say:

> Who knows? Perhaps The Economist *will learn enough from its failures that its next autonomous effort will have clearer directions and will follow a more iterative path. Then Red Stripe will be hailed as a critical learning moment...*

And, besides all that, if it is classified as a failure – and we do have a seeming appetite to classify things *somehow* – Professor Amabile, whom we meet in **The Last Fart of the Ferret** (page 117), says that, '*if people do not perceive any "failure value" for projects that ultimately do not achieve commercial success, they'll become less and less likely to experiment, explore and connect with their work on a personal level. Their intrinsic motivation will evaporate.*'

Dilemmas

- Almost everyone writing about creativity and innovation would agree on the importance of allowing, and attaching value to, failure. It's where the greatest learning takes place. But, if you have a one-off project like this and it fails, it's almost by definition impossible to be pleased about that: personal learning may thrive on failure; innovation teams don't. So what is your position on failure honestly going to be?

Notes – Success

- To take just one example of what people say about failure: Management f-Law No. 57 [Ackoff, 2006] says: 'Managers cannot learn from doing things right, only from doing them wrong'. Professor Ackoff expands on this: 'Doing something right can only confirm what one already knows or believes; one cannot learn from it.'
- Scott Anthony's thoughts are online at [Anthony, 2007].

Stages of the Group

Stewart (typing an email to someone he wants to ring him): *'I'm more available in the afternoon than in the morning.' That's not right, is it?'*

Mike: *'It should be more availableness.'*

Stewart (typing it): *'That can't be right. Are you taking the piss? Are you some kind of Scottish monster?'*

The late Petruska Clarkson (whose CV has to be one of the most extraordinary documents you've ever tried to read on a website), has a lot to say about the stages of group formation and development.

Petruska wrote with equal and unbridled enthusiasm about fame, psychotherapy, the clitoris, organisational change and much more. A simple diagram of hers represents what, in her view, goes on in groups at the outset:

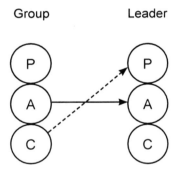

In case it's not immediately obvious, P = Parent, A = Adult and C = Child. The solid line represents the visible, 'social level' transactions that take place within the group (i.e. people relating to each other as adults), and the dotted line represents the subliminal, 'psychological level' transactions that take place. Here the group leader clearly stands in the role of parent. This role, as elsewhere in life, has both positive, nurturing aspects and negative, critical aspects: the latter is most clearly evidenced by young mothers in supermarkets but both can be seen in almost any small girl as she alternately cuddles her doll rather gooily and then rebukes it furiously for some imagined misdemeanour.

The group members relate to the leader, at times anyway, not exactly as children, but with some of the expectations and memories that they had in their early experiences in groups (the most obvious of which will be the family into which they were born). As 'children' they may be playful and free-spirited or sullen and grumpy or polite and well adapted. The group leader relates to the others, at times, as both critical and nurturing parent. The one reinforces the other:

During one visit to Marylebone Road, I heard Stewart announce that he was going to buy himself some lunch. There was to be a group meeting at 12.30.

> **Mike:** 'Will you be less than five minutes?'

> **Stewart:** 'It's only twenty past. I've got ten minutes.'

> **Mike:** 'You've got eight minutes.'

Stewart returned at 12.27, having been down to the canteen and not out to Marks & Spencer's after all.

Elements of this parental role are apparent when Mike talks about his experience as team leader:

> *With hindsight maybe I should have done 3 months in the [Marylebone Road] room and then got us another room somewhere...*

> *I think I should have kept us to time a bit better. One of the first things I tried to do was to give people a sense of urgency. We'd started doing things that we didn't really need to. We got to, 'can we afford to take an afternoon off?' and that was in the first month...*

I didn't make it big enough, aspirational enough. It should be people saying 'this could change my life, this is the thing I'm going to be remembered for'.

What these observations reveal, clearly, is a sense of responsibility for the team's progress and, at times, a sense of frustration at its lack of progress. Depending on your viewpoint and particular experience, you may consider them appropriate concerns for a team leader or you may think that the rest of the team were perfectly capable of managing time-keeping and their aspirations themselves.

The progress of the group, however, followed very closely the pattern used to describe group process by Bruce Tuckman and many others since: namely forming, storming, norming, performing and adjourning, or, if you prefer the rhyme, mourning.

In the forming stage, group members arrive with very clear needs for time-structuring, social intimacy and stimulation, and with well-remembered experiences of what it's like to be in a group and what kind of behaviour is safe. As Gerard Fairtlough said about his early meeting with the team, there was a sense of 'tentativeness and uncertainty'. At this stage, as Clarkson has observed:

Leaders cannot responsibly avoid being leaders if that is the psychological need of the group in its initial phases, just as parents cannot abdicate all structuring and decision making to an infant without endangering it. The task of the responsible leader at this stage involves, therefore, ensuring the establishment of rules, safety, and boundaries. It is necessary to establish dependency before resisting it. Like a parent, the group leader must have the courage to allow himself or herself to be loved, knowing that the ultimate goal of growth and development leads to the loss of this love.

Mike Seery took these responsibilities seriously, establishing clear time structures and setting up social outings and opportunities for the team to have dinner together occasionally. He had made a firm plan for how the team should spend their time during the first two weeks. After that, he said, it was up to the team – though he did carry on planning for a bit longer than that.

As the group 'matured', his role changed. Witness this exchange at the end of March, when he had stepped back a little from his earlier position. His opinion is still clear, but there's room for debate. They're discussing a forthcoming meeting (one of many, as it transpired) to discuss the ideas they had had so far:

> **Tom:** 'I don't think you need a facilitator. We should be able to trust ourselves to think.'
>
> **Stewart:** 'It was helpful having a facilitator [at a previous meeting] though.'
>
> **Steven:** 'I'll do it.'
>
> **Stewart:** 'I don't want you to.'
>
> **Mike:** 'I don't want anyone to be facilitator because it suggests they're not interested in having an idea.'
>
> **Tom:** 'Imagine if we find we can do it ourselves. Then we don't need to go and get one each time.'
>
> **Stewart:** 'There's a multi-million dollar industry in facilitating. They must be there for a reason.'
>
> **Mike:** 'If we're going to do it ourselves, let's do it for an idea that doesn't matter.'
>
> **Tom:** 'I think we should see if we can work together as a team without having someone to hold our hand.'
>
> **Mike:** 'Even if we do facilitate it ourselves, I don't think we should do it tomorrow. We'd need to go away and do some research.'

Notice also that, as was often the case, the principal discussion was had by just three of the team members. Often the team held meetings where contributions were required from everyone and strictly time-limited. But in discussions such as the one above,

Ludwig and Steven (two of the three introverts, along with Mike, according to their Myers-Briggs' profiles) tended to contribute less. You don't hear their voices much in this book because I didn't hear them much in the office. However, that is absolutely not a reflection of their contribution to the project as a whole.

[For anyone who's wondering, the Myers-Briggs profiles were as follows:

Mike	ISTJ	Inspector	11.6%
Steven	ISTJ	Inspector	11.6%
Ludwig	INTJ	Mastermind	2.1%
Tom	ENTP	Inventor	3.2%
Stewart	ENTP	Inventor	3.2%
Joanna	ENFJ	Teacher	2.4%

The percentages represent the proportion of the US population who share each profile. With 16 types available, the distribution 'ought' to be 6.25%. Though, presumably, the figures change from region to region and country to country. There've got to be more Inventors in Scotland. The Scots invented everything. Even Marconi was probably Scottish.]

Mike's eventual frustration with his self-allocated leader/parent role conformed to the eventual letting go that is required. (Tuckman's group process theory says that the leader should let go in stages, moving from an initial, directing style through coaching and participating to delegating and detachment.) Once the group reaches the 'performing stage', appropriate behaviours for the team leader include:

Constructive Behaviours

Lets people get on with it, letting go

Allows people to be leaders

Becomes participant – joining group

Minimum control, maintains some safety boundaries
– though group will usually do for themselves (time,
refreshing, etc.)

Offers praise, positive strokes for being and for doing

Leadership slot is vacated to appropriate person,
though ready to step in if necessary

Says things like, 'Let's experiment with this'

Invites comment and evaluation, allows group to make
choices

Within a wide range of open boundaries says what's
permitted and what's not.

Relaxes, enjoys group

Gives permission to have fun and work

Encourages and validates: autonomy, immediacy,
authenticity, spontaneity, feelings, skills and knowledge

While probably (like others of his generation and nationality) not
reared in a social environment that delivered massive amounts of
unqualified praise, Mike certainly moved towards the approach
shown above, if rather grudgingly. As he said when I talked to him
afterwards:

> At some point I just made a decision that it was too difficult for
> me to manage the team every step of the way. At that point
> I suppose we became less efficient. It was too much work for
> me to be a member of the team and to manage what we did
> every day of the week.

He also said, in late February after the team had been together
for a month, that he could perhaps have recruited an extra person
and had the team working in three groups of two, with him acting
as facilitator. As it was, he felt that 'a heavier touch' was probably
needed 'to keep momentum up'. Still, and instead, he took a step
back.

Perhaps an important point for any group leader to note is that, at a certain point, it's <u>meant</u> to become too difficult and unproductive to try and manage everything. That's how teams work.

Nevertheless, stepping back and allowing the team to decide for itself left something of a void:

> **Joanna:** 'What are we doing now?'
>
> **Stewart:** 'Anything you like.'
>
> **Joanna:** 'Until when?'
>
> **Stewart:** 'Any time you like.'

Here, as so often, Stewart took on the role of challenging the leader or stepping into his shoes (though Stewart believed that Tom and Steven had overtaken him in that role – in which case they were reserved about it when I was present). As early as 16th February (just two weeks into the project) Stewart said to me that he thought that, if the team had come together without a leader, they would be working on an idea by now. Whether that would have been a good thing, of course, is another question.

What the team as a whole perhaps did least well (in terms of managing these developmental stages) was to attend to the mourning or ending stage, where, as in any grieving process, group members have to come to terms with feelings of denial, anger, bargaining, depression, and acceptance. This seems to me a real issue in a business setting, and particularly in a project team setting, where team members' attention inevitably starts to wander as they focus on the vacuum awaiting them on day 183, even though the project will often require that they focus their efforts and attention more than ever on the superhuman tasks required to meet the deadlines that they have set for day 182.

In the case of Project Red Stripe this was a particularly important stage. Team members were due to return to their old jobs in London, China and Germany, although Steven had by now resigned from his position in Beijing and was planning his return home to Hogtown. 'Don't close your options at *The Economist*. Whenever I talk to my old boss I say how much I'm looking forward to coming back' was the advice from one team member to another at this time. Equally, as the idea emerged that the project would continue with, initially, a team of two, there was inevitable speculation about who might be available, or chosen, for the slimmed-down team. This wasn't discussed openly until the very end of the six months. Had it been, it might have become an opportunity to air and share all sorts of issues. Left undiscussed it also had the potential to lead the team down into Tom's inferno.

Although Mike did talk to the team at the outset and towards the end about life after Project Red Stripe, it was also clear that talk of the end was a distraction at a time when the team was working frantically to work out what the end might look like. And get there. This highlights an almost inevitable problem with teams like this: because they are necessarily lifted out of the day-to-day life of the company, they are also, to some extent, cut off from conventional sources of support and advice (like the HR Department).

Dilemmas

- Leaders cannot responsibly avoid being leaders if that is the psychological need of the group in its initial phases. Yet, the very act of having a leader sends a (perhaps unwanted) message to the team about their role and status.

- As with the dilemma about team-building exercises and facilitators identified earlier, there is a tension between maximising the effective contribution of the team leader as an individual team member, and maximising his/her role as an internal consultant/facilitator.

- Teams need to pay careful attention to their closing and winding down, but this inevitably comes when they have least time available to pay attention to anything other than the job in hand.

- Who should manage the team's aspirations and work practices? The team as a whole or the team leader? The former approach is likely to take time and may never happen. The latter can feel controlling and disempowering.

===

Notes – Stages of the Group

- The diagram is taken from [Clarkson, 1991, pp.36-50]. The CV is at www.mind-gliding.co.uk/physis/cv.htm

  If you're over 40, you very probably know this is Transactional Analysis and you very probably hate it. Like many good things (including French cooking and sex) it has been pared down into an over-simplified, reductionist nonsense. But, in my biased opinion, it's still a very useful lens to look through, provided we remember that human relationships are more than a bunch of capitalist transactions and that humans are more than machines, even if we can't agree what or where the ghost in the machine is.

- For more on the stages of the group, see [Tuckman, 1965].

- The excerpt on leadership is from [Clarkson, 1991] p. 211 and the list of constructive behaviours is from page 9.

Leadership

One point that group development theory largely ignores is the possibility of dispensing with a leader or, at least, dispensing with a permanent leader. In the Red Stripe team, as in many others, it would have been possible to rotate the position of team leader weekly or monthly, either randomly or by election. The team could also have elected its leader (perhaps after the first month when things had settled down a bit and people had got a good sense of each other's strengths and skills and personalities). I think this would have required Mike not to stand for election, otherwise he would almost inevitably have been confirmed in his role, both because of his senior status in The Economist Group and because it would be a perceived slap in the face to vote for someone else.

When he talked to me about this point at the end of the six months, Mike observed that 'there were more people that wanted to be led, rather than lead.' But isn't that normally the case? As Gerard Fairtlough might say, that's what the 'hegemony of hierarchy' does for you.

When I asked Javier, the team coach, about this team leader issue, he noted that the team inevitably brought with them the impression of The Economist Group's organisational structure and their status within it. (I couldn't help thinking of the saying: 'bears the impression of the last arse that sat on it...'). For the project founder and champion (and CIO) to have been anything other than the team leader would have been 'cosmetic' and the natural order would have reasserted itself when the team found itself under pressure, said Javier. And, as for having no leader, he felt that one was needed to move the team forwards in order to meet its deadlines.

I mention this issue because it's now widely accepted that organisations should be flatter and less hierarchical, that power should be diffused and devolved and more networked, if they are to be able to respond fast enough to the pressure for continuous change and improvement. In all that has been written about the deficiencies of command-and-control driven organisational structures, there is a clear sense that self-organising teams or workgroups operate best when they use heterarchical or co-operative or 'female' modes of operation. These can include:

- Consensual decision-making rather than 'orders' imposed from above

- Job roles and tasks within the group being rotated or changed to meet current requirements

- Persuasion and engagement replacing the wielding of power and authority

- The selection of leader(s) by the team, rather than having them imposed.

Javier may be right that 'the natural order' would have reasserted itself under pressure. Arie de Geus says something similar when he talks about the reality of decentralisation and empowerment:

> *Few dare to risk the accompanying loss of control. Most of those who dare will show their fears in a crisis. They will recentralise quickly, pulling power back into the centre and into the top. After all, beneath the rhetoric about empowerment, most managers trust themselves infinitely more than they trust anybody else.*

But Arie's aspirational conclusion is rather different:

> *To behave with ecological concern often requires a leap of faith: you will be better protected by harmony and flocking than by territoriality and force of will.*

Dilemmas

- Electing and/or rotating the team leader is 'fairer', more democratic and likely to bring a wider range of different talents to the task. But it's also likely to be inefficient at times and may be no more than window dressing.

- Most managers trust themselves infinitely more than they trust anybody else. But, as Russ Ackoff observes, their subordinates invariably know that they are wrong to do so.

Notes – Leadership

- For more about Group Development Theory see **Stages of the Group, page 50.**
- Writers talking of heterarchical teamworking structures include, amongst many others, [Priesmeyer, 1992], [Falrtlough, 2007] and [Vaill, 1991].
- On empowerment, see [De Geus, 1999, p.169]
- For an explanation of the term 'flocking' see **Flocking** on page 191.
- On managers' self-belief, see [Ackoff, 2006(a), p.9].

Motivations

The team had a conference call with Javier. Javier asked them about their personal feelings and motivations about the project.

The following extracts from their unprepared answers give a distorted and wholly unfair view of why the team members were there. I quote them for several reasons:

> **Steven (who is wearing jeans):** *'I'm hoping that my work will provide potentially an out from Beijing* [after the six months of the project, he was due to return to his job there]*... I'm interested in the glory. I think it's going to look really good on my résumé.'*

> **Stewart (who is wearing jeans):** *'I wanted to learn what it takes to start something... Part of it is to guide me on whether to leave my existing job. I'm a classic geek... Should I develop a separate work personality? My intention is to learn about how to be me.'*

> **Ludwig (who is wearing jeans):** *'For me it's also a personal development thing. I want to learn whether I can work in a team... Shall I go on being a journalist?'*

> **Tom (who is wearing a cravat and waistcoat):** *'I wanted to learn how to do start-ups... My big dream is to be a stand-up comedian and to write comedy... There's a revolution happening in media. It's one of the most exciting times you can even imagine.'*

> **Joanna (who is wearing black and a very high collar and later told me, 'I tend not to wear jeans because I like a degree of formality to get my head in the zone'):** *'I think what I really like is being part of a process... I love this sort of exercise: making things come together... I do like belonging to something. Being part of this thing, with such kudos, is so good on your CV and a real privilege.'*

Mike (who is wearing jeans): *'I wanted to do something I enjoyed more than my old job. I wanted to do something that proved that I can do something other than what I'm currently doing.'*

Now, my reasons for quoting them:

First reason: the team made much of honesty and openness. One of the ten draft recommendations, which were then whittled down to seven for inclusion in the 'not a white paper' was: **Be honest with each other.** There were often times when team members felt that they didn't achieve this goal, which Stewart had named during the first week thus, 'We should be able to say to each other, "You're a bit slack."'

At the end, Mike summed this feeling up by saying, 'The unsaid stuff exploded a few times.' The unsaid stuff was what Tom had stuck under the table in Inferno early on. Mainly, what was unexpressed, I think, were negative feelings that they had about each other. But, in situations like this one, I was struck by the team's remarkable frankness about themselves.

Learning to say the negative stuff about each other in a constructive way, and learning to hear it in an open and non-defensive way, is one of the toughest skills, in my opinion. We have very few role models for it. Few families can manage it. It's a skill that's intrinsically alien to children, politicians, journalists and even most teachers. Yet it's probably at the heart of almost any successful team. This team had that skill in very good measure.

Second reason: there was some debate later on about whether the team should have been offered a financial bonus for a successful outcome, or a share in the resulting business. Everyone except for Ludwig said that some kind of financial incentive would have helped:

Steven: *'It would have been different if we'd all had a financial stake, for sure. Much different.'*

Yet it was clear from the conversation and the websites and blogs that the participants had created as part of their applications, that the opportunity to work on a groundbreaking project like this for *The Economist*, to get away from the routine of their usual jobs and to have a chance of coming up with the next Google was already a massive incentive.

So what was it that led people to look for a further financial incentive? What was it that led Mike to say, '*I got the sense at one point that people were just turning up for work.*'?

Probably it was connected to how the project was going. Had the team members felt that they were on the verge of creating the next Google, they would all probably have been happy with the kudos and happy just to be part of it. Mike had various thoughts on this, including blaming himself and a helpful suggestion which only Tom really took up:

> *I didn't make it big enough, aspirational enough. It should be people saying 'this could change my life, this is the thing I'm going to be remembered for'.*

[I don't agree with him on that. Everybody knew it could change their life. That was the whole thing. If anything, in my opinion, it was *too* aspirational.]

> *Maybe people were too comfortable. I don't think it's anything to do with incentivising. If people had been out of a job at the end of the six months, that would have been an incentive. That's how most start-ups work.*

[I sort of agree with that. It's the problem with intrapreneurship, which is generally defined as the practice of using entrepreneurial skills without taking on the risks or accountability associated with entrepreneurial activities. It is practised by employees within an established organisation using a systemised business model. Intrapreneurial employees are supposed to behave as entrepreneurs, even though they have the resources and capabilities of the larger firm to draw upon and are not exposed to the risks or accountability normally associated with entrepreneurial failure. If people had been out of work, they would have come up with a business, for sure. But *The Economist* didn't need a business. They had a very good one already, thank you very much. In this case, the team found they had to do far more than come up with a business. Which is, in part, why **Lughenjo** and **HiSpace** didn't happen – *The Economist* didn't need them enough.]

Third reason: people at work are just like people at home. They're not very grand. They want to feel OK about themselves, feel wanted, find out what sort of a person they really are, do something they can be proud of, make people laugh, have fun. When I said in an early blog about the team that they needed a mother, I think that's what I meant. Because work has always been a very chilly business. Where do you go for a hug and a wail? They did need someone to make tea for them, but mostly they needed someone to ask them if they were OK and to find out what they wanted. Perhaps I meant that they needed a grandmother. Not like my grandmother who used to wander round the house with a steaming potty. But instead, a wise old babushka. Every team should have one.

Dilemmas

- Honesty, in many situations, including a marriage and an innovation team, can be a two-edged sword. In principle, it is highly to be prized. In practice, it may be sensibly avoided.

- If an innovation project is set up well, the drive for success 'should' be sufficient motivation for the participants. At the same time, not to give participants a stake in the project's eventual success can seem inequitable. Then again, trying to work out an equitable way of giving them a stake in something that hasn't even been thought of yet is almost impossible.

- A classic conundrum: companies that *really* need to innovate are often the ones that don't have time for a project like this one. Those that have the time and resources and are already very successful are probably not motivated to implement the ideas their innovation teams come up with. How do you motivate a company (rather than its individual members) to be innovative?

- How do you bring the spirit of granny into the workplace?

Notes – Motivations

- For more on Javier Bajer see **Coach Class**, page 171.
- Interestingly, it was Stewart who, later, most often named his own concern that the other team members would think that *he* was a bit slack.
- See the online version for a link to the blog about tea-making babushki.

Inspiration

Stewart (after talking on Skype to Steven's friend I Shuen, a web designer, in China): **'She's really nice.'**

Steven: **'She's married.'**

Mike: **'Are we actually sourcing this in China? That's fantastic. I only picked Steven for that.'**

On a bright afternoon in early March I sat in the Red Stripe office. There were only three members of the team there. (Often two of them would go downstairs to the canteen to talk without disturbing the others and sometimes Ludwig would have a long, but working, weekend in Berlin with his family.)

There was a general sense of absorption but not urgency. It struck me as remarkable just how much can be done without leaving a computer. So much, in fact, that I think we sometimes forget that there is still work that *can't* be done in front of a computer. It was more noticeable to me as I was always without a computer, writing with a pen on a piece of paper.

Stewart's main excitement that afternoon was a conversation on Skype with a designer in China. It sounded, apparently, as if she were in the same room. He was momentarily incensed, whilst reflecting on the conversation, that we accept such poor quality telephony as natural. But he's young and doesn't remember when STD meant Subscriber Trunk Dialling or the postmistress in Kinlochspelvie who used to listen in to every call to that end of the Isle of Mull.

That lunchtime and that afternoon a serious question was crystallising about the process. These fine minds had, between them, come up with a process that allowed little room for their intuition or their imagination or their creativity. They recognised this. Joanna noddingly reported a conversation with Tom, in which he had identified that they were just 'funnelling and analysing' without any real creative input.

They were using vox pop – more properly, crowdsourcing – to look for ideas. The team had been divided down the middle about whether this was a good idea and had, in the end, decided to try crowdsourcing not out of laziness or fear of not being creative enough themselves, but because, in Business 2.0, that's what you ought to do. It was also an opportunity to work together and get to know each other as a team on a demanding and time-sensitive exercise – a kind of dummy run for the whole project. As Mike said in his final report:

> Some people had thought that our public call for ideas would yield the killer idea. Others thought that they had it already. And the rest thought that a decent dose of inspirational brainstorming would be needed.

What, I wondered, were the odds of the interested world at large coming up with a better idea than the six of them locked in a room brainstorming, discussing and sharing ideas? In any case, I was now watching the team designing a form and a process for collecting and evaluating other people's ideas. I still wondered if they didn't fully trust themselves. Could a babushka have persuaded them to trust themselves? Of course, it's more of a personal gamble if they rely on their own ideas rather than on the collective wisdom of *Economist* readers. If the latter don't come up with the goods, then how could the team have been expected to do any better themselves? But, then again, the average *Economist* reader probably gave the question five minutes' thought before writing a reply. (Actually, the average *Economist* reader didn't reply at all.)

And on the question of soliciting ideas from the public at large – Dell's IdeaStorm website was launched at around the same time – my guess is that this rich seam is going to be exhausted very quickly. It reminds me of the early days of direct mail when 5% of the people you sent a mailing to would buy your product. Now it's about 0.12%. In five years' time, how many people will respond to this kind of solicitation for good ideas?

The implications of choosing crowdsourcing were surely significant – remembering that one of Mike's stated intentions was to come up with a process that The Economist Group could replicate. There's now no way of knowing whether the team could have done as well or better on their own. I also wonder what would have happened if one of the team had come up with an idea so shockingly inventive and so devilishly ingenious that the rest of the team had all gasped, with one voice, 'Let's do it.'

Much the same questions were raised when the team started looking at how to evaluate the ideas that they would receive. Tom was responsible for working out a process for doing this and, one day, wearing a yellow tee-shirt, he went round the room discussing his thoughts so far with each member of the team individually. (He tended to do this more than the others, who were more inclined to call a brief meeting of the whole team.)

Coming to Joanna, I heard her ask him, 'Do we go for ideas that excite everybody, or do we group them to see that 50% are to do with timeliness or world peace?' Tom answered saying he felt they would group them, do more research, do a presentation on each main idea group and ask a list of standard questions, like 'how disruptive is this technology?' and 'how do people do it now?'. He felt that each presentation should be made to the group as a whole, which would then split into sub-groups of two to discuss the presentation, before reassembling for further discussion.

At the end of their discussion Joanna asked, 'Is that some help? Is that the kind of feedback you need?' (I only once heard anyone else say such a thing.) Was her question the product of a dominant feeling function? Of her being the only woman? Of her lack of assurance about her technical knowledge? Of her sophisticated teamworking skills?

In the end, unsurprisingly, they were less scientific than Tom had imagined at the outset and the issue became one of finding an idea that all the team members could get behind wholeheartedly. For that they needed Javier's help.

Dilemmas

- What are the odds of the interested world at large coming up with a better idea than a small group of fine minds brainstorming, discussing and sharing ideas and purposefully dedicated to finding the best one?

- Do you go for ideas that excite <u>everybody</u> or simply for ones that command a majority? If you can't find one that excites everybody, for how long should you keep looking? Should you set a deadline for that in advance? If you <u>do</u> set a deadline for agreeing an idea, will the team inevitably keep arguing right up to the line?

Notes – Inspiration

- There's more on crowdsourcing in **Open Innovation** on page 105.
- The final report, as usual, is [Seery, 2007: 10].
- Writing in *The Economist* in 1982, Norman Macrae credited Gifford Pinchot III (who sounds like one of those enthusiastically sleek-haired dogs in the Pedigree Chum ads) with inventing the word intrapreneur. Although Macrae was writing more than 25 years ago, many of his ideas about the participatory workplace are as relevant as ever. I recommend the full article [Macrae, 1982]. Macrae quotes Pinchot as saying:

    If we are to get really good problem-solving in our decentralised corporations, we must introduce a system that gives the decision to those who get successful results, not to the inoffensive. Such people will be willing to take moderate risks and will be more concerned with achieving results than gaining influence. These are among the characteristics of the successful entrepreneur. What is needed in the large corporation is not more semi-independent departments run by hard-driving yes men, but something akin to free-market entrepreneurship within the corporate organisations.

Achilles Syndrome

Petruska Clarkson, whom we meet in **Stages of the Group** (page 50), is one of several people to have written about the Achilles Syndrome – or fear of failure worked up into a proper problem. Here are seven characteristics of the 'Achilles Syndrome', as described by Clarkson and summarised by Alan Rayner:

1. A mismatch between externally assessed competence and internally experienced competence, leading to feelings of 'I am a fraud'.

2. Inappropriate anxiety or panic in anticipation of doing a particular task.

3. Inappropriate strain or exhaustion on completion of a task.

4. Relief instead of satisfaction on completion of a task.

5. Inability to carry over any sense of achievement to the next situation.

6. A recurrent conscious or unconscious fear of being found out, and of the ensuing shame and humiliation.

7. A longing to tell others about the fear of being called weak or unstable. This sense of a taboo adds to the strain, loneliness and discomfort.

Some of these characteristics (including inappropriate anxiety when faced with having to speak in public) afflict most of us and I would classify them otherwise: as something to do with the desire to be special and to be seen as special, but the fear of being seen as ordinary. That may be another way of saying the same thing, though: Clarkson suggests that this syndrome has its origins in our upbringing and education, which tend to lay undue emphasis on success and performance in a competitive culture and which neglect basic human needs for love and respect in the quest for superiority.

The result is what Clarkson calls 'pseudocompetence' – apparently advanced skills built on fragile foundations.

I'm not interested in trying to diagnose whether the team suffered from Achilles Syndrome, though I suspect that, providing we accept the rather grand label of 'syndrome', probably most of us do.

Connected to this, I began thinking about the twin towers of specialness and ordinariness when contemplating my shaking hands, flushed cheeks and growling stomach as I awaited my turn to 'say my name and a little bit about me' at a recent workshop. 'This', I thought, 'really shouldn't be such a big deal any more'.

Then, in a recent interview, the 12th Earl of Drogheda reveals that he didn't join a dramatic society at university. 'Now why would that be?', the interviewer enquires. The conventional and anticipated reason (too shy) comes first: 'I think this was because of a mixture of insecurity…'

The second, and rather unexpected, one comes next: '…and fear of not being given star roles.'

Hold it. Fear? Of not being given star roles? That looks like an unusual fear. Even in a world where we discover new phobias daily. But it echoes my conviction that much shyness and holding back reflects not our discomfort at being the objection of attention *per se*, but our grandiosity: our fear that we won't be seen to be as clever, important, noteworthy, funny, beautiful as we think we really are – or could be.

It reflects our unspoken expectation that we should be not just good, but significantly better than the others. So, we're embarrassed to speak in public because we would like to be not just good enough but the finest orator in the land. And the Red Stripe collective clearly wanted a big success, even if they were nervous about saying this out loud. Tom, of course, wasn't. At the outset, he said he wanted a massive success. So did Mike: 'I want something fantastic'. And the team, in an early exercise where they considered what failure would look like, named 'boring', 'incremental' and 'old business model' as aspects of failure. Tom also made the connection with shame: if they failed there would be shame attached to that failure. Of course. Brave to say it, though.

Tom's naming of the word 'shame' is also a reminder of one downside of the very public profile that Project Red Stripe adopted. If the almost inevitable desire to aim high, to go for gold rather than settle for bronze, can become self-limiting when it means that teams exclude modest ideas that might lead eventually to revolution, then it can be all the more dangerous in the glare of publicity, where spectacular success is to be prized even more highly.

The narcissism induced by publicity (and I use narcissism in its pseudotechnical sense rather than in its more common, pejorative sense) has been described by Cornell's Professor Robert Millman as Acquired Situational Narcissism – a form of narcissism that develops in late adolescence or adulthood, and is brought on by wealth, fame and the other trappings of celebrity.

So here, there's perhaps a case to be made for a formal public face for the innovation team. One that keeps the team in the limelight but its individual members out of it.

Emmy van Deurzen also talks indirectly of narcissism when she discusses 'living in tune with your intentions'. She cites the case of someone who wanted to be in control but tended to give up because she could never be <u>fully</u> in control. In Emmy's view, she needed to recognise the 'limitations on being in charge, rather than a striving for absolutes.' Striving for absolutes is the striving for specialness as against a recognition and acceptance of ordinariness.

This recognition of limitations involves both a recognition of quantitative limitations (we can strive to be rich without striving to be the richest person in the world) and of the limitations of reality (in a fantasy world we may be able to fly, drink from the fountain of eternal youth or whatever, but in the real world we very probably can't).

In both cases, we can see the need for some tightening of the brief, some imposition of limitation on expectations, for the innovation team.

Dilemmas

- If you hire people who know a lot about a particular subject, they may have a vested interest in showing that they know *everything* about it. Even if they don't. Hiring people who know less may mean that you get people who aren't embarrassed to admit the gaps in their knowledge and go out and fill them. Or it may just mean that you get people who know less.

- The desire to aim high can be self-limiting if it precludes picking 'the low-hanging' fruit.

- The oxygen of publicity brings in ideas but can induce a greater fear of failure than is necessary.

- Tightening the brief helps team members focus but precludes at least some potential ideas – there's an inevitable trade-off between the two.

Notes – Achilles Syndrome

- The summary of Achilles Syndrome is from [Rayner, 2008].
- On the longing to be special, see **Profitability and Systems Thinking** on page 89.
- On pseudocompetence, see [Clarkson, 1994].
- Lord Drogheda was interviewed in *CAM: Cambridge Alumni Magazine*, Lent 2007 issue.
- The team exercise where success and failure were examined is discussed in **Success** (page 47).
- Professor Millman was interviewed on the subject in *The New York Times*, 9 December, 2001 and in many other places besides.
- The example of the narcissist who wanted to be fully in control is from [van Deurzen: 2002], p.202.

Mindsets

Any book subtitled 'The New Psychology of Success' ought to be enough to have you running for cover. Dr Carol S. Dweck's *Mindset* is an exception, or, at least, the idea behind it is. Apart from introducing me to Alan Wurtzel (who memorably said to Jim Collins, 'They used to call me the prosecutor, because I would hone in on a question. You know, like a bulldog.') it extends attribution theory in an interesting way.

(Though I think the bulldog is not famous for its homing instinct, I absolutely want one with a chisel and a honing instinct.)

Just as Petruska Clarkson in **Achilles Syndrome** (page 71) attributes some of our fear of failure to our upbringing and to what we are told about ourselves and the need to succeed, so Carol Dweck relates our development of a fixed mindset or a growth mindset, in part at least, to our upbringing and the strengths, weaknesses and traits that people attributed to us in childhood.

The characteristics of the fixed mindset include a belief that, 'I'm good at these things and no good at these things, and nothing much is going to change that.' The result is that life becomes a series of opportunities to show off what I know or to conceal what I don't know. I will often resist change and shrink away from challenges in case I get shown up in the process or because I already know that I won't be able to do what is being asked of me.

The characteristics of the growth mindset include a belief that, 'I can learn from just about any situation. I may never be the world's greatest tango dancer, but I can improve.' The result is that life becomes a series of opportunities to grow and learn and I welcome challenges, problems and change for that reason.

Of course, this is a simplistic summary and Dweck acknowledges that splitting the world into two types of people is always misleading. We all share both characteristics. Fortunately, Dweck has brain scan evidence to confirm her hypothesis, which – along with neurochemical and DNA evidence – is the new god. (Which is why Steven Rose, in a review of Edelman's *Second Nature: Brain Science and Human Knowledge*, refers to 'biologists and their philosopher-acolytes'.)

Among Dweck's conclusions, which include the blessed instruction not to teach your child that she is enormously special, or 'the best' at this subject or that sport, are some about business. Dweck talks about the learning skills of the most effective CEOs and the most productive teams, about their willingness to surround themselves with people who know more than they do, about their willingness to do what they think is right regardless of how they will be judged, about their readiness to admit mistakes and to apologise and move on, and about their acceptance of the fact that their company's success or failure does not make *them* a success or failure.

I don't know about the mindsets of the Red Stripe team (although their willingness to join the team in the first place suggests that they were open to the challenge and undaunted by the fear of failure). But it's clear that it might be useful for any team and its members to read *Mindset* and consider how they could learn to be:

- Less defensive about mistakes.
- More open to criticism.
- More willing to tell their story and get feedback from outsiders.
- Less troubled by questions of knowledge, status, authority and rank.
- Less bothered by what each of them is good at or not good at.
- Open to critique, open communication and different viewpoints.
- Open to the idea that relationships between team members can evolve (because the fixed mindset can see not only the individual but their entire world as fixed).
- Open to the idea that problems don't mean deep-seated flaws.

Incidentally, in adding the link from the online version to Carol Dweck's book at Amazon.com I noticed a gizmo which tells me what percentage of people who viewed the book finally bought it. Answer (at the time of writing): a staggering 95%. But much more interesting for me was to learn that 1% of people who had viewed the Amazon. com page then decided to buy *Harry Potter and the Deathly Hallows*. Which seems like a sound decision.

So I couldn't resist trying the same thing with the Bible. I followed the link to the first version of the Bible that Amazon offered me. It was the King James edition. Here I learnt that only 66% of visitors to the page bought the book. Happily for interfaith dialogue though, 4% of visitors to the page ended up buying the Koran instead. But do check the reader reviews of the Bible. They're fantastic. I particularly liked:

> *'The book itself is quite boring. It is frankly a pain to read.'*

and

> *'This particular version is extremely difficult to follow due to what I'm assuming is a translation issue. The syntax is similar to poorly translated Kung-fu movies, but on top of that there are many words that appear to be completely made up. Then there is the disregard for continuity in the story.'*

and

> *'This book was boring; it needs werewolves and lesbians or something.'*

Dilemmas

- While open mindset people are more flexible, less defensive, and so on (as described above), it may be harder to get them to make a decision, stick to it and advocate and pursue it in the teeth of opposition (desirable characteristics if you want to make a good idea happen).

- In the same vein, many successful entrepreneurs are stubborn egomaniacs. But common sense and/or right (on) thinking suggest that a team full of them would be a disaster.

Notes – Mindsets

- Read more about Alan Wurtzel in [Collins, 2001].
- Steven Rose's review was published in *The Guardian* on Saturday 17 February, 2007.
- Dweck's conclusions are in [Dweck, 2006] pp.108-139.

The Straw Man

Tom tended to go round and discuss ideas with, or canvass opinions from, the team members individually. Others preferred to ask everyone when they were all together.

The team had, early on, had meetings where it was felt that time was wasted because people weren't prepared or spoke for too long or confused the business of expressing views, sharing information and making decisions.

The team's solution for this was the straw man, which seemed to work well. The straw man is shorthand for the technique of putting up an idea for discussion early – before it's been fully researched or fleshed out – so that you can get quick feedback from other team members and find out who has useful knowledge they can share about it. Calling it a straw man means that the presenter of the idea is less attached to it and there is less concern about criticising it diplomatically (or at all) for fear of being negative.

The point of building the straw man is to knock it down and rebuild something much better. It's a good place to start, and often provides the impetus you need to get past decision-making paralysis.

As Stewart said, 'I really like the idea of a straw man. It's much easier to say, "This is what I think we should do. What's wrong with it?" than "What does everybody think we should do?"'

Dilemmas:

- You might think I'm making dilemmas up, just for the sake of having one for every chapter. Nonetheless, if you follow the principle that the team reviewing an idea should respect their colleagues' ideas and say three positive things about any idea before criticising it, and if you wish to stay open to new ideas, and if you wish to be seen as an open and receptive cove… you could end up wasting a lot of good time on bad ideas.

Notes – The Straw Man
- There's a good introduction to the straw man concept at www.mindtools.com

Equifinality

Frederick Taylor, the father of scientific management and a modernist to the core, believed that there was 'one best way' to do anything. He was a closed systems man. The ineffably named Ludwig von Bertalanffy, one of the founding fathers of what we now call Systems Thinking, was an open systems man. He proposed that:

> *Every living organism is essentially an open system. It maintains itself in a continuous inflow and outflow, a building up and breaking down of components, never being, so long as it is alive, in a state of chemical and thermodynamic equilibrium but maintained in a so-called steady state which is distinct from the latter...*

He maintained that, in an open system, 'the same final state may be reached from different initial conditions and in different ways'. Which theory is called equifinality – different paths to the same destination.

So there's the science.

Actually there's more. It's called the neo-Schumpeterian theory of complexity and innovation. I mention it mainly because, said right, I believe it can have the same effect as Kevin Kline saying, 'Le due cupole grandi della cattedrale di Milano'. But there's some interesting stuff for aspiring innovators in there too.

Joseph Schumpeter devoted more effort to the study of innovation than any other economist in the first half of the twentieth century. He coined the term *unternehmergeist* to describe the spirit of entrepreneurship that drives technological innovation (which was, of course, a different sort of becoming-animal in the 1940s from what it is now). He argued that innovation was driven by entrepreneurial individuals and, as economies developed and expanded, by large corporations.

Accordingly, he developed a bias in favour of explanations of innovation that were based on the character and determination of outstanding individuals and defined innovations as 'Acts of Will'.

This idea – that an act of will is more important than an act of knowledge or intelligence – is an interesting one. It's also old fashioned. But, though unfashionable, it's still relevant: put six other people in that room on the Marylebone Road for six months and something utterly different would have happened – though they might, using the theory of equifinality, have arrived at the same destination. It's why I've talked at length in some chapters about motivation and incentives and other prerequisites of an act of will (which Fichte says is the primary impulse of Pure Ego, the purpose of which is the fulfilment of a duty or obligation).

Post- and neo-Schumpterians take a different view. Keith Pavitt talks, for example, of:

> Three broad, overlapping sub-processes of innovation... the production of knowledge; the transformation of knowledge into products, systems, processes and services; and the continuous matching of the latter to market needs and demands.

Red Stripe clearly wasn't really in the business of producing or generating new knowledge. The team were overtly looking to see what they could do with what was already out there (which is largely what all Web 2.0 and 3.0 stuff is about) and which is another way of saying 'the transformation of knowledge into products, systems, processes and services'. Where they became inspired, or confused, or changed direction seemed to me when they started matching these putative products, processes and services to market needs and demands (in **Still in Beta**, I've talked about what might have happened if they'd explored market needs first and only looked at products, processes and services later.)

In any case, and in conclusion, my suggestion is that the three processes of innovation identified by Pavitt and the neo-Schumpeterians offer a fruitful way of considering innovation.

Mike Seery, incidentally, refers to IBM's four types of innovation in his final report, which he describes as 'not a white paper in the traditional sense':

Eureka! – true, out-of-the-box innovation

Exemplar – pursuing innovation to build reputation and possibly value

Best of breed – apply proven concepts across the organisation systematically

New to me – apply or adopt changes of value without claiming novelty.

An equally useful framework.

Dilemmas

- Innovation can be driven by individuals with ideas, commitment and determination and it can be driven by an organisation that puts in place the culture and infrastructure to facilitate creative endeavour. Or both. The dilemma can revolve around whether to focus resources on personal development or organisational change.

- Starting with the customer and the needs of the market, or starting with existing products and knowledge and capabilities, may lead to very different innovative outcomes. (Or it may not). It will certainly generate a very different innovative process. Neither way is obviously right, though 'experts' these days tend to prefer the former (market driven) approach.

Notes –Equifinality

- Everything you need to know about Frederick Taylor is to be found in [Taylor, 1911].
- The same applies to [von Bertalanffy, 1968].
- The Kevin Kline reference is to *A Fish Called Wanda*. On a related matter, writing about the eroticism of glossolalia, Trevor Pateman [Pateman, 1998] has said:

> ... the poet and some others are engaged with language in ways
> which might be characterised metaphorically as tactile: the poet
> feels a way with words, almost as if they were touched objects,
> tested for warmth and coldness, hardness and softness. And, indeed,
> linguists happily talk of hard, soft and liquid sounds. But the testing
> (at least for the poet – perhaps this is where the pathological cases
> differ) is also against feelings, so that what is at issue is whether
> a word (as sound or sense) can act as a container – as a means of
> expression – for feelings and emotionally-charged thoughts. If they
> are good containers, then they can contain what is deposited in
> them and the poet has thereby let go of what they contain: a result
> which may occasion relief or depression.

- For more by Schumpeter, try [Schumpeter, 1942]. After reading the manuscript of this book, Gerard Fairtlough talked about Schumpeter to me and he puts Schumpeter into a broader innovation context in [Fairtlough, 2008].

- See [Fichte, 1970]. The idea of prioritising duty or obligation is, of course, shocking to many people in the West in what Vulpian [2008] calls a dechristianised age. It's an interesting question, though, whether overthrowing the icons of authority (class, church, respectability) actually unfetters the ego. In the wake of listening to so many 1968 activists (archetypal iconoclasts) during this anniversary year, it's clear that the most likely outcome is that we substitute internalised authority figures for the toppled external ones. So, maybe, Freud and the superegoists and Eric Berne [1961] and the Parent/Adult/Child brigade didn't have it so wrong after all.

- The extract from Mike's report is [Seery, 2007, p. 5].

Oblique Strategies

I'm not sure who to credit here. You probably know of Brian Eno and Peter Schmidt's Oblique Strategies. Loosely based on these is a list of ten strategies for start-ups, which I found on Sean Murphy's blog. They are strategies to help get a team 'unstuck'. The first line is the oblique strategy, with some additional commentary of Sean's and mine:

☐ **A line has two sides**

Sean's suggestion is that the team construct a diagram to represent the forces holding the system at its current equilibrium point (keeping the situation stuck). They draw a vertical line down the middle of a piece of paper and then draw arrows representing the forces working for and against the change you want to make. Each arrow is assigned a 'strength' by its length. Initially most teams focus on strengthening the forces working *for* them, but it's often as fruitful to consider how to diminish the forces working *against* them.

☐ **Abandon desire**

Fear and desire, it seems to me, are second cousins: both relate directly to what might be going to happen in the future. Sean says that it's as important to let go of fear as greed. This could be fear of failure, fear of the bigness of the becoming-whale-of-an-idea, fear of humiliation or being 'seen'. Associating fear and desire is revealing in other ways: the eighth of W. Edwards Deming's 14 points for management was the need to 'drive out fear'.

☐ **Abandon normal instructions**

According to Sean, most successful breakthrough teams don't 'break all of the rules,' just the ones that are truly getting in their way, and they understand the risks and likely consequences. This is an important balance to get right. As Charles Leadbeater observes in *Living on Thin Air*, 'we are scientific and technological revolutionaries, but political and institutional conservatives'. I think 'normal instructions' relate here principally to the mechanics, norms and habits of working.

☐ **Accept advice**

I talk a lot about this elsewhere and particularly in **Alexander Bain and the Fax Machine** (page 163).

☐ **Back up a few steps. What else could you have done?**

Here the suggestion is to keep decision records. Russell Ackoff suggests that a decision record should incorporate the following items (and that it's more important to document when you decide not to do something so that you lay the groundwork for tracking both errors of commission and errors of omission):

- A brief statement that justifies decisions, including likely effects and outcomes.

- The assumptions that the decision was based on.

- The information, knowledge, and understanding that went into the decision.

- Who made the decision, how it was made, and when.

- Be dirty

- 'Go Ugly Early' – a product marketing aphorism that I talk more about in **Creativity and Innovation** (page 39).

☐ **Be extravagant**

Waste money to save time, waste time to save money, waste either or both to improve morale or customer satisfaction. Which raises the question of who was the customer here. At times it was Mike, but mostly it was the The Economist Group Management Committee. Inevitably, it was hardly ever the users/market for the eventual idea. But there was a noticeable change of temperature, while **Bavaria/ Lughenjo** was being developed, when the team considered the customer as African children who couldn't go to school or the NGOs whom they were trying to work with and support.

☐ **Breathe more deeply**

Don't mock. It has a calming effect and gets more oxygen to your brain for clearer thinking.

☐ **Change ambiguities to specifics**

If you have deferred a decision, try and set a value on one or more particulars you have been avoiding just to see if you can at least find a feasible solution.

☐ **Change specifics to ambiguities**

Sometimes a team gets locked on a particular process or price point or other decision that in fact doesn't have to be made today. You may get prematurely anchored to a particular value that's not important instead of asking what customer benefits are affected by this variable.

From my time observing Red Stripe this is a really useful starting point for any team. (As far as I know, they weren't aware of this list, but they certainly debated and applied some of these principles from time to time – including '*How would I explain this to my granny?*', see **Rules and Values**, page 114.)

Dilemmas

- Innovation teams should, by definition, break rules. But, being composed of institutional conservatives, they need to be clear about which ones to break.

- If you abandon fear, desire and greed, are you abandoning the motivations most likely to get you a good outcome?

- Not really a dilemma this one. More of a resolution. Many of the Oblique Strategies offer ideas about how to handle dilemmas. Decision-making is often hampered by our habit of looking for a single solution. So the suggestion here is simply to value dilemmas as moments of creative possibility, rather than looking on them as something that one gets stuck on the horns of.

Notes – Oblique Strategies

- There's also a full list of Oblique Strategies on the BBC website. See the electronic version for the link.

- Sean Murphy's blog is in the **Biography**.

- While many of Deming's [Deming, 1982] more practical points (e.g. 'move towards a single supplier' and 'break down barriers between departments') were absorbed into the TQM revolution in the 1980s and 1990s, others – like 'drive out fear' – received only lip service. Curiously, organisations that take an official stance against bullying may often still be run by individuals who fall back on aggressive or coercive tactics when under pressure.

- *Living on Thin Air* is [Leadbeater, 1999].

- The great Systems Thinker, Russell Ackoff, has been rebuked for saying the same thing more than once. Which seems a little harsh when you consider that a) we all do it and b) few of us have as much to say about almost anything as he does. For more, see [Ackoff, 2006a and 2006b].

- I recently discovered that everyone except me knows that 'go ugly, early' is based on a principle adopted by lonely hearts: save yourself the anguish of pursuing the beautiful but unattainable stranger all evening and make a play for the plain one right from the start. The idea is nicely developed by Danny Schmidt (www.dannyschmidt.com):

> Then a father, full of wisdom
> Said I learned when I was young
> That a pretty face ain't worth the chase
> Go ugly early, son
>
> ...But when you gaze at her beside you
> You best rid yourself of pride
> Til the colors of your feathers
> They match the color of your hide
>
> Cause in the question of the conquest
> You might find it's just as true
> That the girl that you chose early
> She went ugly early, too

Incubating Innovation

In setting up Project Red Stripe, *The Economist* unquestionably did the right thing, according to specialists who know a lot more about innovation than I do. Jeneanne Rae and her colleagues analysed sixty recent innovations in the service industry, including in-depth interviews with key team members (How do they do that? I managed to watch *one*. A bit.) She wrote about her conclusions in *Business Week*. Her fourth (and 'specially important') principle is:

> *Techniques and structures that counterbalance the forces of risk aversion.*

She explains that big enterprises are large because they're successful and success is a barrier to innovation. Why try something new and risky when what you're doing now works? If it ain't broke... (which is the point I make in **Motivations** about the group's eventual decision not to go ahead with the **HiSpace** idea, see page 62).

One of the techniques and structures that she proposes to deal with this situation is as follows:

> **Form a special petri-dish environment where new concepts can grow.** *Pitney Bowes has a concept studio designed to explore opportunities far afield from its existing lines of business. IBM has a similar unit, called 'EBO' for Emerging Business Opportunities. This approach minimises distraction to the ongoing business and permits concentration of special innovation skills. Successful projects are then sold back to the business units.*

A petri-dish environment is what *The Economist* got itself with Project Red Stripe. Furthermore, the ubiquitous Dave Pollard quotes disruptive innovation expert Clayton Christensen describing IBM's survival in the face of waves of disruption from advances in computer technology as being down to its use of innovation incubator units.

There are two reasons for doing this, according to Christensen:

1. Nurturing innovation requires different skills, different resources, a different benchmark of success, a different management style, less aversion to risk, and a different focus from the mainstream business.

2. Innovation can be a distraction to the mainstream business, threatening the processes and attention to traditional customers that have made the mainstream business successful.

Commenting on Jeneanne Rae's article, Tom Foale rightly observes:

> Demands from existing customers fuel sustaining, not disruptive, innovation. Disruptive innovation can't be analysed for growth potential because it creates new markets, so it usually gets filtered out either explicitly (it doesn't meet growth needs) or through internal pressure for staff to perform. Most businesses whose development teams have created disruptive innovations let them go elsewhere -- look at Xerox for an extreme example.

There's more on this in **Reading Matter** on page 134.

So *The Economist* did the right thing. Whether they did the thing right is what I'm discussing everywhere else in this book.

Dilemmas:

*   If it ain't broke… don't fix it ~ but, if it ain't broke, these days, it probably will be soon enough.

*   Disruptive innovation, like equilibrium-threatening evolutionary changes, tends to get filtered out. Filtering it back in tends to be painful and, of course, disruptive.

Notes – Incubating Innovation

*   For the *Business Week* article and Tom Foale's later comments, see [Rae, 2005].
*   This whole question of nurturing innovation relates to one of Clay Christensen's principal points in *The Innovator's Dilemma* discussed in **Reading Matter**, page 134, and in [Christensen, 2008].
*   Dave Pollard's blog is *How to Save the World* – listed in the **Biography**.

Profitability and Systems Thinking

Stewart: *'The thing that was really difficult was cutting the brief down.'*

Noted commentator and Guardian columnist Jeff Jarvis, who had had breakfast with the team in March and been impressed by them, later said on BuzzMachine,

> I have to say that I was disappointed with The Economist's Project Red Stripe in the idea they ended up with and in the fact that it is not yielding a product.

> ... they ended up, I think, not so much with a business but with a way to improve the world. Their idea, 'Lughenjo,'... wasn't intended to be fully altruistic; they thought there was a business here in advertising to these people, maybe. But still, it was about helping the world. And therein lies the danger.

> This gives me hope for the essential character of mankind: Give smart people play money and they'll use it to improve the lots of others. Mind you, I'm all for improving the world. We all should give it a try.

> But we also need to improve the lot of journalism. And one crucial way we're going to do that is to create new, successful, ongoing businesses that maintain and grow journalism. We need profit to do that.

> So I would have thrown another requirement on Project Red Stripe or any media company's innovation incubator: that they start a sustainable – that is, profitable – business.

Interesting points from a respected commentator, but themselves laden with assumptions and preconceptions.

First, Jarvis here, and at greater length in his article, equates *The Economist* with journalists and journalism. Red Stripe tended throughout to dissociate itself from journalism, to leave the journalism business to the magazine. Red Stripe was working with all The Economist Group brands and businesses and customers as a starting point and was, wisely I think, looking far outside the box for ideas. I'd say it was visionary of the group and of the project team to allow themselves that latitude, especially in the face of concerns that the *Economist* brand could be damaged, that they had an innovation process already and, more mundanely, that it would be difficult to find people to do the jobs of the six team members for six months. There's a peculiar convention, outside the department store and hypermarket, that businesses should really only do one thing – 'core is king' could be the continuing slogan of this mindset.

Second, Red Stripe came up with a profitable and sustainable model in **Lughenjo** (though, admittedly, they began by thinking of it as a not-for-profit business). Their reasons for dropping it were only incidentally to do with profitability. In fact, Mike Seery's conclusion, *pace* Jeff Jarvis, was that 'we don't have a working prototype because we got hooked up on money – that was the thing this project was supposed to avoid.'

Third, any analysis of anything which juxtaposes 'helping the world' and 'improving the lot of journalism' and sees the former as a danger to the latter seems alarmingly mechanistic and possibly back to front. As Sheldon Rovin says in a piece on Systems Thinking:

> *... we live in an age of unprecedented possibility... Deplorably, though, you wouldn't know we live in such an age, judging by the way our politicians, corporate leaders, so-called experts and other authorities go about trying to solve our serious problems. Influenced largely by the thinking of Aristotle, Descartes and especially Newton, that the world is a mechanism awaiting explanation through analysis, taking things apart and studying the parts to understand the whole, they use a piecemeal, get it done fast approach that at best temporises, but more often worsens the problem*

Neil McIntosh in his own blog, responded to Jarvis thus:

> *... 'profitable' is quite a narrow definition of success. I prefer a looser definition of innovation; the successful introduction of something new. 'Success' can mean profits, or reputational*

benefit, or better user experience, or saving the world, or all of those things at the same time. Profits are just one – albeit frequently very important – measure of success.

But one thing that struck me from all this was this: not all innovation needs to be radical. Indeed, most attempts at clean-sheet, big bang innovation fail.

The innovation that normally yields results is the kind that arrives in a light drizzle; small, incremental, building on work done by yourself or others, utterly un-noteworthy to all but the geekiest observer.

'Success' is covered elsewhere, but his comment on innovation is nice. We tend to experience innovation as revolution (for example, with the car, the telephone, the iPod, the Internet) because of the way those innovations revolutionised our lives. In fact, of course, the technological innovation that enabled those *experienced* revolutions was gradual and piecemeal. This is an important thing for innovation teams to know and remember. Several small steps are the most reliable path to a major change. Red Stripe explicitly sought to avoid incremental change. At the outset, Mike said 'I tend to steer people away from the incremental approach'.

Suw Charman had another angle on this in her blog about Project Red Stripe:

Innovation, like all other forms of creativity, never comes out of nowhere; it comes out of all that's been before. All the things you've read, conversations you've had, scenes you've witnessed, and – most importantly – all the work other people have done. Creation requires giants upon whose shoulders we can stand; we cannot do it in a vacuum. Indeed, sitting down with a clean sheet of paper, trying to conjure a killer idea out of nowhere is only going to end in tears, mainly of frustration.

When it comes to technical innovation, any developer worth his or her salt will tell you that the best way to come up with a winning idea is to think about a problem that irks you and that you want to solve.

Jeff Jarvis (whose blog started this chapter) responded with this thought:

> So I think there is a need sometimes to take people who are ready to make change and to build some sort of net around them to experiment without fear or the crushing pressure of corporate inertia. Maybe The Economist should have sent their team off not with the magnificently open challenge – create something innovative and of the web; that was it – but instead with a problem to solve and a few hypotheses to try out.

Dilemmas

- A focus on profitability may be good for innovation, but it isn't necessarily helpful for creativity. On the other hand, since we're talking about business, almost any focus that isn't on profitability might be seen as a distraction. On yet another hand, Tom Peters was just one of many to assert that businesses should focus on delighting their customers, allowing the profits to follow in their wake.

- Most innovation is incremental and emergent in nature, even if it looks revolutionary to the customer. As a result, looking for 'quantum leap' innovation may be self-defeating if it assumes technological or other changes that haven't yet taken place. On the other hand, an innovation project predicated on 'quantum leap' innovation won't get anywhere if it simply looks at incremental change.

Notes – Profitability and Systems Thinking

- The extracts from Jeff Jarvis's blog are from BuzzMachine (see **Biography**) and linked from the online version of this book.
- A potential solution to the problem of reconciling viable business models and altruistic objectives is suggested in The Art of Strategic Conversation [van der Heijden 1996, p.41].

- A detailed analysis of the wrong-headedness of the orthodoxy that philanthropy and capitalism cannot comfortably co-exist and a much more nuanced approach to the subject can be found in [Hampden-Turner & Trompenaars, 1993].
- Sheldon Rovin's comments are taken from an email sent by him in June 2007.
- Neil McIntosh's blog is called CompleteTosh (see **Blography**).
- Suw Charman's blog is called Strange Corante (see **Blography**).
- The Tom Peters aphorism is from [Peters 1999].

Other people's conclusions

It's easy to argue with other people's conclusions. Which is one very good reason why I'm trying not to draw too many myself.

But they do make a good springboard.

Mike Seery draws seven conclusions in his 'not a white paper', written at the end of the project. The first of them is the recommendation that you should 'have a strategy for team selection'. As he says, 'this may sound really obvious'. Which it is and it isn't. His recommendation goes on to suggest not just any old strategy for team selection, but this one: 'consider getting people to group themselves into small teams as part of the selection process'.

Now this is an interesting idea and he expanded on it when I asked him at the end of the project what he would do differently with hindsight:

> I would probably select the team differently. It took a lot of our time to get the team working in any sense together and to have any kind of shared view of what we were trying to do. So I'd probably get people to form themselves into a team around an idea. Even if their idea wasn't necessarily one that we used, at least they'd have worked together and at least there would be some kind of cohesion.

> I'd say to the applicants: 'You need to go and find three other people who'll work with you', maybe given them some money and a week to put their team together. I'd take the team that seemed to work together best... The hard bit about this project is that people found it very hard to work together in a team.

Richard Daft among many others has talked of the need for an idea champion, who will build support for a particular idea or innovation and gather around her a small group of like-minded people who have agreed to work with the idea champion if the idea gets the go-ahead. Gerard Fairtlough also stresses the importance of this approach at W.L. Gore and describes the process in that organisation whereby project champions gather around them co-workers who support and endorse the project. 'As support accumulates for a project', he says, 'it becomes better and better defined: for instance, as people skilled in project accounting join the team, as well as those with relevant marketing or technical expertise.' While Dave Pollard argues that 'it makes more sense, in creating a Natural Enterprise, to start by identifying the people you want to make a living with, rather than the type of business you want to create.' A Natural Enterprise is one that sets out to find a need and fill it (which I've discussed further in **Peter Drucker and Gary Hamel**, see page 160).

Given the circumstances in which Project Red Stripe was set up (i.e. that people were co-opted for six months and someone else was found to do their jobs), this kind of approach would probably not have been feasible. Suppose Stewart had gathered around him three or four colleagues whom he had persuaded to back his good idea, it would have been tricky to take this group as the basis of a project team – it would have decimated the Economist web support team. However, as part of a general move towards creating an innovative culture where ideas are had, evaluated and passed on to a development team, it could be very useful. Fairtlough also discusses this problem, saying that 'projects inevitably compete for key people and other resources, and there is rivalry between them. However, priority choices are made heterarchically.'

It seems to me that bringing people from different departments (editorial, marketing, web support, advertising sales, etc.) and from different countries was a crucial part of the process of trying to draw in ideas from as wide a range of sources as possible.

When afterwards I talked to Javier Bajer, the team coach, he suggested the following solution to the problem of how to pick team members:

'Make the call for ideas heart-driven or belief-driven', so that people are invited not to say they'd like to be on the team because they have useful skills and a lot of knowledge and some good ideas, but to submit a proposal that really embodies a personal dream or aspiration – thus prioritising commitment and the will to act over knowledge, experience or anything else. He suggests picking a good mix of people from this pool and then working hard to form them into a team.

Javier's point here is that when people go beyond feeling committed to an idea to becoming attached to it, then any criticism of the idea becomes criticism of the idea-owner.

I suspect you can argue this one both ways. It may be that undiluted attachment to an idea is exactly what's needed to drive it forwards and that the role of other team members can be to ask salutary questions and help the idea-owner see alternative solutions and possibilities. For example, even though Tom later said, 'I knew what I wanted to do even before we started the project and that held me back', he would have said something different if his enthusiasm for his idea had helped to get it adopted by the whole team. Perhaps, too, preventing criticism from becoming personal can be a task for the team facilitator, rather than something to be avoided by disallowing ownership of ideas.

As always, I suspect you can do it any way you like. You just have to manage the issues that come up.

Going back to team selection, maybe it would have been possible to get the team members early on to form themselves into sub-groups that each endorsed one of the different ideas that the team members brought with them at the outset. But this would have been at odds with Mike's third recommendation: 'People shouldn't own ideas'. (There's more on this in the chapter with the wickedly punning title **Coach Class**, page 171).

Mike's other conclusions were:

Be open at your peril. His point here was that the dialogue they opened via the call for ideas was time-consuming, difficult to manage and sometimes threatened to blow them off course.

Talk to people outside the team – meant less in the sense of getting expert external advice (which they did enthusiastically in the research phase of **Bavaria/Lughenjo**) than in Javier's proposal for getting energy into the team (discussed in **Coach Class**, page 171).

Understand the trade-offs with verification – choose your moment with care when deciding to discuss your ideas with the senior management team.

Don't try to produce a business plan (in a six-month project) – a preoccupation with commercialising the idea can be distracting, he says. Talking to me at the end of the project, he combined this with the previous point when he said:

> We need to recognise what happened with the intervention from The Economist Group. Even though it was kind of conversational and not telling us what to do, the moment we had the idea it started getting changed, because we told people back at the Group about it. We should have probably stayed true to our brief and just developed it anyway... We might have had a working prototype by now rather than worrying about how it made money. Because the idea doesn't care whether it makes money or not.

And, finally, **agree a single outcome.** Here he nods at the whale thing:

> There is a clear difference between an outcome and an idea. For example, creating a search engine is not an outcome whereas 'indexing all the world's information' is. The outcome does not need to be set in stone for the duration of the project but it serves to focus people on coming up with different ways of achieving it and along the way ideas will be thrown up that may turn out to be 'the big idea'.

Just so.

Dilemmas

- Choose team members for their different skills, backgrounds and experience and you may lose a lot of time trying to build them into a team. Choose team members who already work together well and you may narrow the range of enquiry and exclude much-needed skills and points of view.

- Prioritising motivation over skills (or vice versa) during team selection raises a similar dilemma to the previous one.

- Getting 'too attached' to an idea makes it harder for people to change their minds and think flexibly. But it also enables them to fight for it and commercialise it in spite of negativity and resistance from other quarters.

- Take your plan to the Board too soon and you may have the stuffing knocked out of it by pragmatists whose only concern is profit. Take it to them too late and you may find you've wasted a huge amount of time if you can't get their approval. (This dilemma, like many of the others, obviously begs other questions. The answer here may be to say that the innovation can be spun off into a separate business if it doesn't win the Board's approval as discussed in **Reading Matter**, page 134.)

Notes – Other People's Conclusions

- Mike's report (not a white paper) can be seen at www.projectredstripe. com (follow the link from the 19 November, 2007 blog post).
- The Daft ideas are set out in full in [Daft, 1992].
- On W. L. Gore, see [Fairtlough, 2007, p.88].
- Dave Pollard's blog, How to Save the World, is referenced in the **Biography**.
- Tom's idea (and the others) are explained at some length in **Those Ideas in Full** on page 208.

Siphonophores

I'm going to tip-toe into the lion's den of Cultural Theory to think about the dynamics of the team a little further.

I've talked about people's preferences (when it comes to work and working together in teams) in psychological and psychometric terms (see **Stages of the Group**, page 50, for more on their Myers-Briggs' profiles and on theories about the development of the group). I've also talked repeatedly about the business of choosing or allocating a leader and the role of the team leader.

But Cultural Theory talks about the five solidarities, which are the five ways of organising things (or the five ways that people organise themselves, or the five ways that people think about how they organise themselves, or whatever). These are:

- Hierarchical
- Individualist
- Egalitarian
- Fatalistic
- Autonomous

Now if, like me, you are simultaneously delighted and appalled by random new ways of dividing up humanity, your pulse may have quickened slightly at this point. If you're already starting to find fault with this scheme, hang on and hear the background:

The background lies with Mary Douglas, who developed Grid and Group theory. Think of Grid as an axis on a graph. At one end lie strict laws and externally imposed regulations governing all kinds of behaviour. At the other end, things are pretty lax. Then think of Group as the other axis. At one end, people are long-term members of well-defined groups and social groupings. At the other end, people belong much more loosely to groups with much less well-defined boundaries. Here's a picture:

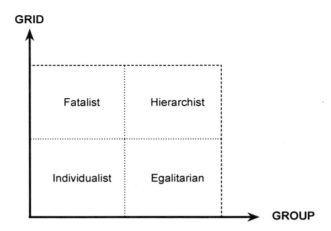

- In low Group and high Grid, people are (or feel) controlled from outside but have (or feel they have) little control over others via the organised social groups and networks of which they are a part. In this situation, you tend to become fatalistic – resigned to whatever shit 'they' or 'the universe' are going to dump on you next. This is the position of people who find themselves impassively at the bottom of the hierarchical heap. People in this group aren't particularly exercised about any specific risks and threats, because a lot more bad stuff is just round the corner and going to happen anyway.

- In high Group and high Grid, you have a well-organised, highly structured, hierarchical society or organisation where people know their place and behaviour is tightly prescribed. Threats to the order of things are seen as the main risk.

- In low Grid and high Group, you find co-operative, egalitarian, heterarchical set-ups and preferences, where the rules are made by the group and not imposed from the outside. The main threat here is felt to come from unfairness and inequality, which might threaten the egalitarian arrangement.

- In low Grid and low Group, you tend to find that unconstrained individualism and market forces prevail. Remember that Mrs. Thatcher said there was no such thing as society. Again, the particular threats and risks that people will be concerned about are ones that threaten the set-up: the imposition of regulations and controls that undermine individual freedom, for example.

• Somewhat outside (or else at the centre of) this pattern, sits the hermit, who operates autonomously of both Group and Grid.

This is a terribly simplistic version of something that people have written whole books about. It relates, equally simplistically, to Triarchy Theory, which says there are three ways of organising (rather than the above five): hierarchy, heterarchy and responsible autonomy. These three relate, although perhaps not as tidily as they first seem, to some of Cultural Theory's solidarities.

If you've been paying incredibly close attention and are reading the book backwards, you will have noticed a connection with Georges Dumézil's assertion (mentioned in **Reading Matter**, page 134) that sovereignty has two poles: the magician-king, who uses capture, bonds, knots, webs and nets, and the jurist-priest who governs by treaties, laws, pacts and contracts. We could say the magician-king uses Group and the jurist-priest uses Grid.

Next up is Spiral Dynamics, which needs to be treated with caution. Although it's not a cult (I know this because it says so very clearly on one of the two leading SD websites), it has split into two variants, each with its own website and expensive lawyers (much like NLP). It has also been called 'The Theory that Explains Everything', which should be enough to warn us to approach with the same care that we would give to a Portuguese Man o' War (which is a siphonophore not a jellyfish, for those who care about such things, and whose tentacles are ripped off and used in combat by the gelatinous blanket octopus). Spiral Dynamics uses special colour coding (entirely unlike those aura analyses which tell you whether you are to be an ascended master or a bicycle in your next life). It proposes a series of 'Levels of Existence', which go something like this:

Level 1: Automatic - Motivated by physiological needs – with no real sense of time, reasoning or self-awareness.

Level 2: Tribalist - Sense of tribe rather than a sense of self. Sees existence in polarised terms: good and bad. Emphasis on taboo and superstition.

Level 3: Egocentric - Clear awareness of self. Aggressively individualistic approach to life. Characterised by the hero archetype.

Level 4: Saintly - Rules predominate. Obedience to these rules is the price of a secure, lasting life. Accepting the order of things is essential.

Level 5: Materialist - This level is concerned with exploring and controlling the environment using whatever methods are appropriate. Pragmatic and Machiavellian. Manipulate and expect to be manipulated by others. Go it alone if necessary.

Level 6: Personalist - Relating to others and being with others is the most important thing. Group membership is greatly valued, as are consensus and democracy.

Level 7: Cognitive - Here the emphasis is on information, knowledge, competence and science. The best leaders are those that know the most. Values are derived from current information.

Level 8: Experiential - Values experience and understanding over knowledge and information. Trust and respect are essential. Coercion and restriction are resisted and domination avoided.

These levels are seen to apply to different periods in human history (suggesting an alarmingly teleological view of the West in the 21st Century as the pinnacle of human social achievement) but are also used - in a spiralling way - to describe social behaviour in groups (where all of these levels can apply now). More constructively, we could see the team (any team) and individual team members passing through some of these stages during the life of the team, and individual and group tendencies to occupy one particular level as both productive and restrictive.

So how can we use and apply these theories? Apart from noticing which of Cultural Theory's solidarities group members and the group as a whole tend to occupy, we can consider how they think differently about their environment and the risks, threats and opportunities that they face.

The individualist approach, for example, might involve seeing customers, colleagues, the Internet and the outside world as resources to be exploited in the development of a big new idea that will eventually be profitable and advantageous. Others (team members, other teams, outsiders) might seem like the biggest risk if they were to steal or co-opt the idea.

The egalitarian approach might tend to prioritise working heterarchically with others in and outside the group. An egalitarian might emphasise a concern not to 'exploit' external resources but to preserve the delicate balance of their environment (in the broadest social and cultural sense of the word) over just making money.

The hierarchical approach might prioritise the establishment of systems and procedures and favour openness between team members to ensure that nobody went off and pursued avenues or ideas that might threaten or weaken the effectiveness of the team as a whole.

An awareness of some of these tendencies might help any team when it is thinking about (for example) whether to encourage members to work at home/out of the office, whether to have a formal or elected leader, how to discuss and debate ideas and make decisions, and how to approach idea-gathering and harvesting.

Similarly, an awareness of the different levels of Spiral Dynamics might throw up some interesting discrepancies between intentions and reality. For example, in **Rules and Values** (page 114) I talk about the fact that the team focused a lot on trust and respect when it was agreeing a list of things they should all commit to. This sounds like Level 8: Experiential. However, in practice, the team was often more concerned (inevitably) with rules and procedures or winning consensus or acquiring and making use of information and knowledge (which are characteristics of different Levels). Understanding the Levels could shed light on these gaps and discrepancies.

Dilemmas:

- Almost any way of carving up humanity into groups and types seems simplistic and arbitrary, but many can offer insights. Why choose any one of them over the others and, indeed, why use any of them at all, if they tend only to lead to fruitless (in project terms) introspection?

- Pick team members representing a diverse selection of levels and solidarities and expect disharmony and disagreement but, perhaps, a richer outcome? Or pick team members with similar dispositions, get working together faster and more easily, be more productive but perhaps miss opportunities seen only from other viewpoints and perspectives?

Notes – Siphonophores

- See [Douglas, 1982] for the original explanation of Grid/Group theory and Michael Thompson [2008] for a wonderfully discursive analysis of the solidarities at work – he moves effortlessly from discussion of regional tensions and political institutions in the Himalayas to a consideration of Unilever's 'Dove' toiletries and 'Frish' lavatory rim blocks.

- Gerard Fairtlough [2007] talks at some length about Cultural Theory and Triarchy Theory and their application in organisations.

- Spiral Dynamics has its own 'gateway' website at www.spiraldynamics.com to help you choose which of the two paths explains everything best. In amongst some alarming-sounding stuff like Holonics and Humergence, there is also a very interesting discussion of value systems and their memetic transmission, for those who still subscribe to Richard Dawkins' theory of memes as units of cultural transmission, as set out in The Selfish Gene.

- Javier Bajer's Leadership Alignment Tool (LAT) – described in **Coach Class** (page 171) – is designed to uncover discrepancies and gaps of exactly the sort talked about here.

Open Innovation

Dr Henry Chesbrough had a good idea about innovation and wrote a book about it. In fact, the idea was so good that he wrote three books, several articles and launched a website about it. Along the way he interviewed hundreds of people who confirmed his hypothesis that there are two sorts of innovation: open innovation and closed innovation. These can be given capital letters thus: Open Innovation and Closed Innovation. Both can also be followed with the word paradigm, for good measure.

To save time, I'll use his own summary of the Open Innovation paradigm:

> Open Innovation is the use of purposive inflows and outflows of knowledge to accelerate internal innovation, and expand the markets for external use of innovation, respectively. [This paradigm] assumes that firms can and should use external ideas as well as internal ideas, and internal and external paths to market, as they look to advance their technology.

Dr Chesbrough's idea is described as 'pathbreaking' on the jacket of his book, where several wise people are quoted fulsomely endorsing his idea. Scott Cook, Chairman of the Intuit Executive Committee, goes so far as to say that the book is both seminal and practical and 'provides the how-to for revving up your innovation engine for leaps of profitable growth'. I'm hopeful, confident even, that no-one will describe the present book in that way.

In the Closed Innovation paradigm, a company uses insiders to have ideas, some of which it develops and commercialises in-house, using the profits partly to fund further research and idea-generation in-house. In the Open Innovation paradigm, in case your attention drifted during the bit about purposive inflows, the same company gets ideas from wherever it can and takes them to market through a combination of internal and external channels.

Red Stripe used a combination of both paradigms: insiders drew ideas in from outside, but then had their own idea, which they discussed widely with outsiders, before setting about commercialising it internally. It could, of course, have done any of those things differently. I don't have a view on whether it should have (though Dr Chesbrough does). I just think that innovation teams may find it useful to think carefully about this question at the outset.

But another thought in Dr Chesbrough's book caught my attention. In the foreword, John Seely Brown talks about two sources of learning: learning by doing and learning while waiting. John Seely Brown clearly likes this idea too, because he's put the whole of his foreword on his website, which is indicative of the closed loops in which this kind of discussion takes place. But it's another revealing thought for an innovation team. Certainly the Red Stripe team found and had ideas while they were waiting to decide which idea to take to market and while they were soliciting ideas from outside. But their **Bavaria/Lughenjo** idea evolved considerably in the course of 'doing' the business plan, talking to partners and getting ready to make their formal presentation to the GMC. It was from this 'doing' process that the final **HiSpace** idea emerged.

I think it's fair to say that some of the ideas that emerged from doing were more practical and practicable than many of those that emerged from the earlier waiting process. So, there's perhaps a case to be made for 'doing something', even at the outset, because it may reveal ideas of a different order.

Once again we can view the Red Stripe approach as a combination of the two. But the outcry that greeted their decision not to publish the ideas that were submitted by outsiders (and which was, generally speaking, based on an objection to a private company soliciting money-making ideas and then keeping them to itself) may have concealed a more important issue – namely that if they had allowed the 'world' to kick around and discuss the ideas that were submitted, they might have found that much of the process of evaluation, sifting, analysis and development of those ideas could have been done for them by people who, collectively, knew more about their viability than the Red Stripe team ever could.

But then, of course, the problem remains that Red Stripe would never have actually owned any of the ideas.

While we're on the subject of learning while doing and the team's conversations with NGOs and other experts who were likely to be involved in the **Lughenjo** idea, I should mention the Delphi technique. I was alerted to it by a *Harvard Business Review* article called *The Wisdom of (Expert) Crowds* by Robert Duboff. The technique, which is not unrelated to scenario planning, is rather like an amplified focus group. You recruit two dozen or so experts on a particular topic and ask them to evaluate possible developments, trends and outcomes in a chosen business or technology area. (There's a lot more to it than that – an independent facilitator then summarises their thoughts and they have another round. And so on. There are lots of rules, which necessitate the hiring of expensive consultants to oversee the process.) I suppose it's also related to the Prediction Markets idea, which the Red Stripe team had discussed at the outset and were encouraged to pursue during their idea harvesting process. As I've said elsewhere, involving the experts eventually led Red Stripe to reject **Lughenjo** and it's possible that the earlier, formal involvement of such a group might have helped them home in on a workable idea. But, of course, that would require that they had first decided which mountain they were going to climb. For sure, Red Stripe were in the lucky position, as an *Economist* team, of being able to get the attention of experts whom others might have found it more difficult to talk to.

Before we leave the Open Innovation paradigm, I'd like to mention another way of thinking about all this that's been around a lot longer. In 1997, Eric Raymond, talking about the open source software movement, came up with the term 'the cathedral and the bazaar', which is constantly evolving into a book. The former represented the conventional method of using a group of experts to design and develop a piece of software (though it could apply to almost any large-scale creative or innovative work). The bazaar represented the open source approach. This idea has been amplified by a lot of people, notably Don Tapscott and Anthony Williams in their book Wikinomics and on their website and blog of the same name. Wikinomics, being the commercialised arm of The Wisdom of Crowds, of course has its opponents and detractors. It's not a panacea and plenty has been written about the foolishness of crowds. Bruce Schneier's essay on the psychology of security is one elegant example of this. But Eric Raymond himself is also quoted in a compelling article by Nicholas Carr as saying that 'one cannot code from the ground up in bazaar style. One can test, debug, and improve in bazaar style, but it would be very hard to *originate* a project in bazaar mode.' In the same vein, Raymond is also quoted as saying, 'The individual wizard is where successful bazaar projects generally start'.

Project Red Stripe had six fine individual wizards, unsure of how far to trust their own wizardry and how far to turn to the wisdom of the crowd.

Dilemmas

- Open vs Closed. You can use insiders or outsiders; your own ideas or other people's; your own money or other people's. With the latter, there's always going to be less ownership and less control. But more room.

- Thinking vs Doing. Trying to implement one idea may inspire other ideas, but settling on an idea too soon may close down other options. Time-tabling is important.

- Crowds are collectively wise. But they are also collectively more limited and unimaginative than some individual wizards.

- Recruiting experts can ensure that you draw on the best minds in the business but may also ensure that the outcome resembles a camel (designed by committee).

Notes – Open Innovation

- Henry Chesbrough's book is [Chesbrough, 2003] and his website is at www.openinnovation.net

- John Seely Brown's website is at www.johnseelybrown.com
- The outcry was on Slashdot (see **Biography**).
- The Wisdom of (Expert) Crowds article is [Duboff, 2007].
- You can read more on the Delphi Technique in [Stuter, 2008].
- The Cathedral and the Bazaar book is [Raymond, 1999].
- The Wikinomics book is [Tapscott & Williams, 2006] and the website is www.wikinomics.com
- Bruce Schneier's essay is [Schneier, 2003] and there's more about him in **Still in Beta**, page 110.
- Nicholas Carr's article is [Carr, 2007].

Still in Beta

I mention Bruce Schneier's article on the psychology of security in **Open Innovation** (page 105). On the face of it, our general inability to make sense of the modern world shouldn't have much to do with Project Red Stripe. But it does.

Schneier identifies the different financial accounts that we keep in mind when performing different trade-off calculations. For example, cinema-goers who had previously bought a $10 ticket were asked whether they would buy a replacement ticket if they found they had lost the first. 46% would. A comparable group who were on the way to the cinema but had not yet bought a ticket, were asked if they would still buy a ticket if they opened their wallets to find that they had lost a $10 note. 88% would.

Talking to the Red Stripe team over lunch one day (about the selection of a 'good cause' for the eventual project), we compared the press coverage given to one death in a train crash with that given to any of the 140 or so children killed in road accidents in the UK each year. Our view of good causes – AIDS orphans, famine victims, maltreated pets, etc. – is also notoriously subject to perceptual bias.

Returning to Schneier's article, he quotes the following words from Daniel Gilbert's exquisitely headlined article, *If only gay sex caused global warming*. Gilbert nicely explains why the human brain is so poorly equipped to make reliable decisions when assessing different risks:

> *The brain is a beautifully engineered get-out-of-the-way machine that constantly scans the environment for things out of whose way it should right now get. That's what brains did for several hundred million years—and then, just a few million years ago, the mammalian brain learned a new trick: to predict the timing and location of dangers before they actually happened.*

Our ability to duck that which is not yet coming is one of the brain's most stunning innovations, and we wouldn't have dental floss or 401(k) plans without it. But this innovation is in the early stages of development. The application that allows us to respond to visible baseballs is ancient and reliable, but the add-on utility that allows us to respond to threats that loom in an unseen future is still in beta testing.

All of this by way of a preamble to Red Stripe's deliberations over a target group or 'market' for their business. Where relatively simple 'interest' equations were involved in deciding what kind of Internet business would be most worth pursuing, far more complex equations became necessary when debating the relative worth of plans to offer better education to children in the third world (the most needy), to children in the first world (the most influential decision-makers of the future), to women (mothers of the poorly educated children), etc.

While the team actively solicited ideas about what they should do, they did not solicit ideas about the group(s) for whom they should implement those ideas. Should they have invited an archbishop, an aid worker, a genetic researcher and others to pitch for a particular target market? I doubt it. But, for me, there was a noticeable change of temperature when I first heard Joanna insisting to the group that they should stop discussing their ideas in a vacuum and consider whom they would benefit and how. I had felt the same myself when she said to me early in March that she was determined to ensure that whatever idea was pursued was grounded in a real need felt by *The Economist* community which, she said, would make it sustainable. She said that the others would have to justify the idea to her and, in so doing, sounded clear and sure of herself. Though, afterwards, she observed that saying that sounded a bit grandiose or arrogant, because the others were all clever people.

In any case, it's possible to end up with a market that you cannot hope to serve, or an idea that nobody wants. Or, as Mike reports David Laird saying to the team at one stage, 'although there may be a gap in the market, the key is whether there's a market in the gap.'

Dilemmas

- A deserving market may be motivational, even inspirational. But it doesn't necessarily make for good business – as we can deduce from observing the investment priorities of any large pharmaceutical company. How do you value a commercial priority against an ethical one in business?

- If you're going to focus on deserving markets, should you wheel in archbishops and others to help you decide which is the <u>most</u> deserving?

- Even if you find a gap in the market, is there a market in the gap?

===

Notes – Still in Beta

- The references are to [Schneier, 2003]. Bruce Schneier (currently Chief Security Technology Officer at BT, and many other things besides) is a chocolate box of extraordinary information. If you thought you weren't interested in security and cryptography and security, have a look at his Crypto-Gram Newsletter (www.schneier.com/crypto-gram.html). Among dozens of other delights in the current issue, I couldn't resist the following:

  > ### EMail After the Rapture

  > *It's easy to laugh at the You've Been Left Behind site (www.youvebeenleftbehind.com), which purports to send automatic emails to your friends after the Rapture:*

  > *"The unsaved will be 'left behind' on earth to go through the 'tribulation period' after the "Rapture".... We have made it possible for you to send them a letter of love and a plea to receive Christ one last time. You will also be able to give them some help in living out their remaining time. In the encrypted portion of your account you can give them access to your banking, brokerage, hidden valuables, and powers of attorneys' (you won't be needing them any more, and the gift will drive home the message of love). There won't be any bodies, so probate court will take 7 years to clear your assets to*

your next of Kin. 7 years of course is all the time that will be left. So, basically the Government of the AntiChrist gets your stuff, unless you make it available in another way."

But what if the creator of this site isn't as scrupulous as he implies he is? What if he uses all of that account information, passwords, safe combinations, and whatever *before* any rapture? And even if he is an honest true believer, this seems like a mighty juicy target for any would-be identity thief.

And -- if you're curious -- this is how the triggering mechanism works:

"We have set up a system to send documents by the email, to the addresses you provide, 6 days after the 'Rapture' of the Church. This occurs when 3 of our 5 team members scattered around the U.S fail to log in over a 3 day period. Another 3 days are given to fail safe any false triggering of the system."

- The gay sex article is [Gilbert, 2006].

Rules and Values

At the outset, the team agreed three rules:

1. don't use the toilet (the one in the office).
2. don't always sit in the same seat
3. don't send emails across the table

Asked to share something positive about the previous week, all the team members but one talked about personal/family experiences, rather than work:

Tom: on holiday in Morocco, had visited a dead warlord's estate

Joanna: had stayed at a Landmark property in Scotland

Stewart: in his work had become proud of what he has achieved

Steve: had said goodbye to China, where he noted that Chinese people never hesitate to ask other people for a favour, except from foreigners.

Mike: had organised a birthday party for two-year olds

Ludwig: had organised an outing with his daughter and wife (until 3am) and resolved to do it more often.

Asked to come up with a list of things that they would all commit to, the team formed into two groups.

The first came up with a long list including: honesty, no booze at lunch, being open with each other, being bold, being ready for criticism, expecting to upset the GMC, supporting each other, being unafraid, remembering that they were lucky to be doing this job, not compromising.

The second team suggested: being reflective, focusing on the positive, developing a meritocracy, transparency, trial and error, taking ownership of the project, putting family first.

The lists were summarised as follows:

- Be open with each other and the outside world
- Be tolerant
- Be honest with each other and yourself
- Stay loyal to each other
- Make a difference
- Be reflective

Finally they were narrowed down like this:

Value	Explanation	Example behaviour
Stay committed	Stay true to what we agree as a team	Keep engaged even if you don't get your way
Be open	Be honest and open with each other	LAT call with Javier
Take ownership	Do what you say you will do	You're looking after the baby
Be respectful	Consider others' feelings; give everyone a chance	Considering how others would like to hear the message you are giving

For a project team of this sort I'm still struck by the 'touchy-feely' quality of this list of things they wanted to commit to. In many ways it seemed untypical of the team and noticeably ignored issues like when and how hard they should work and how much time they should take off. Perhaps it would have been useful to bring the list up to date from time to time to reflect the issues that later emerged in the group. Perhaps drinking at lunchtime sometimes would have promoted fructifying stuff. And in any innovation team, perhaps some of the following oblique strategies (discussed, naturally enough, in **Oblique Strategies**, page 83) would be interesting:

- Ask people to work against their better judgement
- Be extravagant
- Call your mother and ask her what to do

- Discard an axiom
- Display your talent
- Do something sudden, destructive and unpredictable
- Do the last thing first
- Faced with a choice, do both
- How would someone else do it?
- How would you explain this to your parents?
- Make an exhaustive list of everything you might do and do the last thing on the list
- What wouldn't you do?
- You don't have to be ashamed of using your own ideas.

Dilemmas:

- What does coming up with 'a list of things you can all commit to' do? On the face of it, it's an excellent idea. The team reminded themselves of it from time to time. Inevitably, they didn't keep to it fully. Might it be useful to come up with a list of things you cannot commit to? Or that you don't agree about? Or rules that you don't accept? There is shadow/inferno stuff in this list, inevitably. Should it be openly explored?

- How do you balance the pros and cons of allowing or vetoing drinking at lunchtime? Or mind-expanding drugs? (See **Creativity and Innovation**, page 39.)

Note – Rules and Values

- See **Coach Class** (page 171) for an explanation of a LAT call.

The Last Fart of the Ferret

In *Creativity Under the Gun*, Amabile, Hadley and Kramer describe how time pressure has a negative effect on creativity unless the pressure is felt to be meaningful and is delivered in a form where individuals can work largely on their own and in a focused way. Where it's unproductive is when there's just too much going on, too many competing demands and pressures, too many distractions.

Creativity under time pressure, the authors maintain, is most likely to happen when people feel 'as if they are on a mission'. In the absence of any time pressure, they argue that people in an innovation team need to 'feel as if they are on an expedition', which comes closer to the idea of drifting or wandering around, which I explore in **Drifting, Angst and Pan-ic,** page 29). This sense of being on a mission or expedition also reminds me of Tom's euphoria at the outset and occasionally later on.

What Amabile et al. are talking about is motivation, of course. And, specifically, they're talking about what they call intrinsic motivation, which Professor Amabile elsewhere defines as 'authentic', as opposed to the extrinsic motivation produced by promises of a bonus or threats of redundancy. I'm not at all sure about this distinction. What about the motivation to look cool, to get a better job after completing the project successfully, to become famous as a result of delivering a triumphant new business to *The Economist*? Where's the boundary between intrinsic and extrinsic? Why should we try to create a boundary at all? (I'm afraid the answer to that is simply that 'blur' makes less good copy – and sells less well – than 'black and white'.)

The team members were equally unclear about this motivation thing. At different times, several of the team members explicitly said that they would have worked harder or longer hours if they had been offered a share in the eventual business. I don't know how true this was. They all seemed to work hardest when they sensed that their mission was possible and less hard when they felt it was going nowhere. They also worked hardest when presentations and other key deadlines were looming. Though we need to distinguish between working hard to complete a defined process – like preparing a business plan or a presentation – and working hard to be creative – which is a much more elusive skill, as noted by every writer or artist who endlessly displaces creative work, choosing instead to do the washing up or a thousand other humdrum tasks.

Returning to intrinsic motivation, the factors that Amabile says enhance intrinsic motivation include: challenge, freedom, resources, work-group features, supervisory encouragement and organisational support.

Challenge is about getting a good fit, but not too good a fit, between the employee's skills and the task. (This relates to my discussion of who was chosen to do what job.)

Freedom relates to freedom over means but not ends. Specifically, Amabile says that 'creativity thrives when managers let people decide *how* to climb a mountain; they needn't, however, let employees choose which one.' Project Red Stripe could hardly have been given a broader brief than 'creating an innovative and web-based product, service or business model'. (Tom one day recalled the cry attributed to many, including David Ogilvy and Pontus Nyström, of 'give me the freedom of a tight brief'.) It's possible to see the first couple of months for the Red Stripe team as having been spent deciding which mountain to climb. But then again, would the Group Management Committee have been well placed to tell them which mountain to climb?

 The important thing seems to be, as Amabile et al. say, that the time constraints appear reasonable and that, as far as possible, they be imposed by the team itself, rather than from on high. This is at odds with one of my favourite ideas about creativity, which was developed by Taiichi Ohno, father of the Toyota Production System and an inspiration to many Systems Thinkers. In an interview with an *Economist* journalist (and which I have never been able to trace), he reportedly likened creativity in a survival culture to the last fart of the ferret. When a ferret is cornered it emits a powerful stench like a skunk, and employees, he said, when facing closure of the company, would come up with some of their most creative ideas. [Incidentally, if you search for 'last fart of the ferret', Google will rather coyly ask you if you meant 'last fruit of the ferret' – a delightful possibility which, sadly, produces no results if you accept the suggestion.]

But, to come back to the business of creativity itself, Amabile et al. suggest that creative thinking results from the formation of a large number of associations in the mind, followed by the selection of associations that may be particularly interesting or useful. This process of juggling ideas like balls is a playful process and it was noticeable that the team quickly abandoned some of its more playful activities under the pressure of time constraints. As Mike Seery notes in his report on the project:

> However, as early as February, team dinners and outings were delayed or rescheduled, because we were so concerned at using the time to work on concrete ideas. In doing this we unwittingly removed a key element of what allowed us to recharge our batteries and remain fresh and excited about the project.

Incidentally, though they didn't reinstate team dinners, they did in late March, at the instigation of Javier the team coach, begin to go out for lunch in twos and threes to build better relationships between them. Funny that, having sat round a table together all week, people should need to get up and go and sit round a different table to build better relationships. But that's context for you. And movement.

Dilemmas

- Set deadlines and create a sense of urgency or give people the time and space they need to explore in a relaxed environment without unnecessary pressure? If the answer is that different people respond best in different contexts, how do you decide which approach to prioritise for your team?

- Offer financial incentives to participants or deliberately avoid them?

- How do you work out who is best placed to decide which mountain the team should climb? If you don't trust the team to decide for itself, what signal does that send?

- Give the team the freedom of a tight brief or the freedom of a wide one?

- Continue to encourage 'unproductive' play, even as the team approaches the end of the project, or use it only at the outset to foster creativity and team cohesion?

Notes – The Last Fart of the Ferret

- First references are to [Amabile et al., 2002]
- Professor Amabile talks about authenticity in [Amabile, 1998]. She has done further longitudinal reference studies on 'creativity in the wild', not cited here and available from Harvard Business School.
- See more on the team members' thoughts, especially about extra remuneration, in **Motivations** (on page 62).
- Ohno is quoted in [Nakane and Hall, 2002].
- The quote from Mike's report is from [Seery, 2007, p. 8].

Markets

On 27th March the team agreed that their three top priorities in terms of markets that they were aiming at should be children, women and the third world (the last came soon to be called 'philanthropy'). These had been whittled down and refined from a shortlist of four: 'education, charity, women and leisure'. The decision was reached at Javier's instigation to help the team move forwards at a time when it was wrestling with which idea to choose. As Joanna had been saying from early on, focusing on their market would bring a different perspective from focusing on an idea.

It wasn't that simple, though. Every time they got close to narrowing down the options further they encountered the same sort of problem. The next day (28th) they held a meeting to discuss these three markets and I felt what you might call, if you were that way inclined, 'the energy in the room' ooze away. Just as it had, according to the team, when they'd had an earlier out-of-the-office brainstorming session about ideas with Sally Bibb and David Laird. Exactly the same thing would also happen a few days later at a further meeting held to explore these markets. For now, here are some exchanges from the discussion they had on 28th March:

> **Tom:** 'I didn't actually vote for kids.'

> **Stewart:** 'I put kids in as third because there wasn't anything else.'

Or again:

> **Stewart (summarising):** 'These three ideas are in the category of good – doing good for people.'

> **Tom:** 'I think they're more in the category of doing.'

> **Stewart:** 'If categories are not the way to cut it down, what is?'

Or again:

> **Ludwig:** 'What do we want? To have a fully fledged site... a service... or what?'

> **Mike:** 'Hard to say what we want without knowing the first step.'

Asked by Javier how to say in one word how they each felt at the end of this unproductive discussion they said:

> **Steven:** 'Frustrated.'

> **Mike:** 'Frustrated.'

> **Joanna:** 'Stuck.'

> **Ludwig:** ' I want more openness, less tiptoeing. There's no spark.'

> **Tom:** 'Bullish'

> **Stewart:** 'Enjoying the argument.'

Asked if they all shared an ultimate objective, Stewart responded immediately, 'No.'

Mike followed up: 'We don't have a shared view of what the problem is that we would solve for each of the three areas (children, women and the Third World).'

Later in the conversation, Javier asked the simple, but acute, question: 'Why would you want to make kids cleverer?'. Stewart didn't blink before answering, 'I dunno'. And I agreed with him.

Always I felt that becoming–whale-of-an-idea was getting in the way. Moving forwards meant accepting that they'd got the right idea. But they couldn't be sure that they had. Was it 'The-One-Big-One' as Riddley Walker would say?

So Javier invited them each to find a situation they were so angry with that they really wanted to change it. As luck would have it they found it the following week.

Dilemmas:

- Looking for quantum, not incremental, innovation; faced with multiple possible markets and ideas; team members inevitably having different views – how could the team harness the drive and enthusiastic commitment needed to push the project through when they were all perfectly clear that they could just as well be working on an entirely different idea?

Notes – Markets

- For more on Joanna's view on identifying a market, see **Still in Beta** (page 110), and for more on the meeting a few days later, see **Anger** (page 124).
- Riddley Walker is the eponymous hero in [Hoban, 1982]. The-One-Big-One is Nuclear Fission and The-One-Little-One is Gunpowder.

Anger

Stewart: *We all gave each other permission to have a go at each other, but nobody really does.'*

In sessions like the one described in **Markets** (page 121), it felt as if there was something missing. It seemed to me at first that the difficulty was a lack of enthusiasm for the ideas and markets. Team members just weren't sufficiently fired-up about any of them. And that was, to some extent, true. But it became apparent that some of the team, at least, were deeply persuaded by the idea of helping to achieve universal primary education or revolutionising charitable giving or enhancing financial literacy skills.

Another aspect to the lack of energy was anger. Anger, of course, should mean fireworks. But, unexpressed, it can present itself as boredom or depression. In this case, the unexpressed anger seemed to involve resistance by some team members to the others' preferred idea or market or solution. This simmering and largely unspoken, even unacknowledged, resentment came to a head at a meeting on 3rd April at Mike's house where, as he says in his not-a-white-paper, 'A real split opened up in the team and over the course of the following 24 hours it got very close to becoming permanent.'

By this time the team had refined and whittled their ideas down to two: helping to get all young children access into primary education and helping children with poor financial literacy.

As I arrived, they were talking about children. Each of them was to be given five minutes to present and talk about themes, ideas, facts and problems they'd been researching over the last few days. Joanna would write up a summary of each presentation on a flip chart with a red pen.

Stewart went first and talked about levelling the playing field for disadvantaged kids, about giving them role models, about improving motivation levels and about putting learning into context. 'Is that the sort of thing you wanted?', he asked.

Mike: 'It's fine. But let's concentrate on what you've found rather than trying to reach conclusions.'

Joanna had come with a lot of statistics. 22% of Iraqi children don't attend school. There will be 18 million African AIDS orphans by 2010. 91% of 12-year-olds in the UK have a mobile phone. Steven had something similar: there are 250,000 child soldiers in the world. Nearly 5 million kids die of malnutrition each year. He also observed that the problems of children in the developed world 'don't tug at me'.

Tom talked about the problems of disadvantaged children in the West and the emerging social underclass. He identified problems like a lack of role models, a lack of social skills and a lack of time spent with their parents.

Ludwig focused on the problems caused by a lack of financial skills and reported that 62% of 12th graders in the US had failed a financial literacy test, at a time when children were having to make more financial decisions with a long-term impact than ever before.

Lastly, Mike talked about opportunities to develop, create and package coursework for school children after describing the range of problems with curricula in different countries and some of the more innovative solutions that were being found, in Mexico for example.

In summary Mike noted that they had three key areas now: helping children in the developing world, improving financial literacy among children and making learning fun. (This was one more than the two ideas they had arrived with: financial literacy and universal primary education.) He also asked if they needed to narrow their focus again. 'Are child soldiers and child mortality issues for *The Economist?*'

- - - - - -

Now Mike invited each of them to say what, in all this, they were angry about (reflecting Javier's question the previous week.) Here's what they said, in brief:

Stewart: 'We need to get children more interested in what they're doing.' *He didn't look angry to me.*

Tom: 'We're not equipping First World kids with the skills to survive in a globalised world.' *He didn't look angry to me.*

Ludwig: 'Only banks and the finance industry are doing anything to help kids' financial literacy. There's a need for an independent actor.' *He looked fairly angry.*

Mike: 'Children don't want to take an active role in deciding who their leaders are.' *He, too, looked fairly angry.*

Joanna: 'Children end up with all kinds of problems because of the impact of adults on the world. They need more information about food, health and so on. But children are better equipped to assess that information when they're in a supportive environment. Let's do that.' *I couldn't tell if she was angry.*

Steven: 'There's a lack of access to education. There's violence, bullying and gender discrimination in schools. We should enable First World children to help Third World children.' *He looked convinced but not angry.*

I don't know about you, but none of these things makes me angry. I think they might if I were a better person. But I can quite easily get angry about children of primary school age fighting civil wars or making my clothes instead of going to school. In any case, it's not that easy to bring anger about world affairs into a meeting like this one. It's always easier to find it closer to home.

The team then split into two groups for half an hour, at Mike's suggestion, to try and tighten each of these points up into a punchy statement.

Downstairs Stewart, Tom and Joanna were discussing whether helping children achieve their full potential was a smart enough idea for Red Stripe. Stewart asked Tom what he was writing and Tom replied 'I'm just thinking.' Stewart responded, 'Oh, that's how you think. We're doing teamwork for half an hour and you're writing on your own.' Here was the sort of frustration or anger you might well expect of a group working in each other's pockets day in and day out.

After lunch they presented the results of their deliberations in the two teams. Each person had a condensed version of their earlier statement, as follows:

Ludwig: 'Stop kids getting ripped off by improving their financial literacy.'

Mike: 'Allow kids to create a better world by giving them the tools to make conscious political decisions.'

Steven: 'Get all 120 million remaining children in the world into primary education.'

Tom: 'Help disadvantaged children achieve their full potential by empowering them through knowledge, activity and community.' He later changed this to: 'Help poor kids take control of their lives.'

Stewart: 'By 2020 halve global truancy.'

Joanna endorsed the others in her group, not having realised that Mike wanted each of them to prepare an individual statement.

Then they tried to decide which of the above list of distilled aims (there were now five) they should discuss and in what way they should discuss them. After an hour of talking around this question, Mike said, 'Do we want to vote on it?' Ludwig said, 'These things are at different levels' (which was true), and the voting question was by-passed. Eventually they decided on a written vote on the order in which the five statements should be discussed. Each team member was given three votes.

The results were:

> Get all 120 million remaining children in the world into primary education – 11 votes.

> Allow kids to create a better world by giving them the tools to make conscious political decisions – 9 votes

> Help poor kids take control of their lives – 8 votes

> Stop kids getting ripped off by improving their financial literacy – 5 votes

> By 2020 halve global truancy – 3 votes

This was followed by a SUN only session. For the first theme (universal primary education), ideas mentioned included:

- Stop war
- Use itinerant teachers
- Share teachers
- Open source teaching materials
- E-doption
- Pay children to go to school
- Give money to relevant countries
- Build schools
- Work with the UN
- Put courses on mobile phones
- *Economist* radio in sweatshops
- Get Nike to pay for schools

Similarly good ideas were discussed for theme number two. It was then decided that only the top three aims would be discussed, meaning that Ludwig's idea (and it was his idea consistently) about financial literacy wasn't going to be discussed. At this point I left and the team continued into the evening with the meeting ending in angry dispute as the team 'hit a brick wall' centring around which ideas would be discussed and taken forward. Ludwig, for example, felt that brainstorming about world peace was pointless. Steven felt that his language was disrespectful.

Their internal blog recorded only the bald statement:

> **'Apr 3, 2007 6:30pm**
>
> *Ludwig disagreed with the rest of the team on the usefulness of the brainstorming session today.'*

It was now that the almost permanent split noted earlier by Mike opened up. But, with Javier's help, they moved forwards and settled on two ideas: financial literacy for kids and getting all children into primary education. Interestingly, these were the two ideas they had started with on the cantankerous day at Mike's house.

Sometimes things go round and round and seem to get nowhere. That's what I saw at the meeting at Mike's house. I've described it in some detail *not* to rub the participants' noses in it (who hasn't been part of a frustrating and apparently circular argument at work or at home?), but to highlight the convoluted process that may be required to get any group of people to agree about something as important as this.

Some would say that we should give equal value to going round and round and seeming to get nowhere and to getting *somewhere*. But this is less obvious in business, where 'progress' and 'outcomes' are the order of the day. It's also clear that logic and decisiveness can easily be lost when people fear that their work is threatened by other people's agendas. They tend to become defensive and lose their sense of mutual purpose and the excitement that goes with it.

Dilemmas

- Without a full-time facilitator or coach, how do you allow the expression of pent-up frustration or anger without threatening the fabric of a team?

- When time is short and co-operation essential, how do you get people to work together for the greater good, when that means sacrificing their own ideas, projects and visions? In a non-hierarchical setting, what do you do when time runs out and no agreement has been reached?

- If anger is normally generated by personal experience and anger is needed as part of the energy that will drive a team and its ideas forwards, how do you get a team to lift up its eyes and survey the distant horizon?

===

Notes – Anger

- Mike's comments are from [Seery, 2007, p. 12].
- By October 2007, the education situation in Iraq appeared to have deteriorated. UNICEF reported that 'just 28 per cent of Iraq's graduation-age population took their exams at all – 152,000 out of approximately 642,000 children aged 17.'
- In case, like me, you don't know: 12th grade is the final year of secondary education in the USA.
- SUN-only sessions are explained in **Reading Matter**, page 134.

Preface – Sally Bibb

When Mike Seery told me about his idea to set up Project Red Stripe I thought what a wonderful opportunity it presented for The Economist Group. Not only did it open up the possibility of the development of an innovative idea for the web but it also presented a rare opportunity for organisational learning. Indeed it has been, and Andrew Carey has done an excellent job of uncovering and unpicking the process that the team went through, so that others will be able to learn about how to create innovative teams and cultures.

However, learning and knowing how to extract learning from any given situation is not always that easy. The world of work encourages *doing* not *reflecting* and *learning*. And when you only have 6 months to complete a project, with the eyes of the world as well as your own management on you, it undoubtedly feels pressurised at times.

I first got to know Mike Seery about 6 years before Red Stripe. He impressed me with an openness and ability to reflect and learn that I rarely see. He also has a collaborative style of leadership and he is a good listener. All qualities that made him the ideal person to take on this formidable task. Sitting in his office when he had just had the go-ahead for the project I was reminded that he was a person who was strong enough to provide the leadership and focus whilst being secure enough to allow the team freedom to create. I think it was Gerard Fairtlough who said that a leader's job was to provide 'true North' and then let the team get on with it. Of course Mike had the challenge of not knowing where true North was other than being a 'wow' web idea.

It was fortunate that Mike has the qualities I describe above as he was undoubtedly to draw upon everything he knew to be able to succeed. The challenge was formidable and, I imagine, probably underestimated by all concerned. He not only had to meet the expectations of The Economist Group Management Committee but he had a good number of colleagues and strangers watching him too. Some were very supportive and rooting for him. But inevitably there were others who were watching with a critical eye and ready to jump on anything that they did not perceive favourably. On top of that, Mike had assembled a team of people who had high expectations of their own. Some of them had made not insignificant sacrifices to be part of the team. It was important to them. So, whichever way you look at it, the stakes were high. Mike was a man exposed and, a bit like a premier league footballer, if he played well he would be adored by many, but if he made mistakes he would be jeered at and ostracised by the watching masses.

One of the tricks of creating a high performance team and delivering an innovation project is to pay enough attention to the task, the process, the team and the learning. When we are up against a very tight deadline as they were, it is very easy to get sucked into the task at the expense of all else. It is counterproductive to do that. The Red Stripe team were aware of this and tried hard to make sure that all aspects were attended to. Gerard Fairtlough and Javier Bajer helped them to understand, and stay conscious to, the task, the process and the team. David Laird and I worked with them on the process and task too and, as this book shows, they were serious about finding ways of working that would enable them to succeed. They created a learning culture, and learned that it is a prerequisite for an innovation culture.

I spent several hours with Mike and the team during the lifecycle of this project. It struck me that there were a number of different challenges and questions facing him and the team, including:

- How can a leader from a traditional organisational culture create an environment where his team (also from that culture) could become a high performing one within a very different paradigm (and within 6 months!)?

- How can that leader straddle the two worlds effectively throughout the duration of the project and reintegrate into the 'mother' culture afterwards?

- How can the team maintain their resilience when the very nature of their task means that they will have failures before they can have any successes?

- How does a team of people who have never worked together achieve such a challenging task in such a short time?

- To what extent and how does the leader and the team interact with the sponsoring organisation – what are the pros and cons of that?

- How can senior managers from the sponsoring organisation encourage and support the project when it also demands of them a very different 'contract' and way of working?

And finally, probably the most important question:

- How can the people concerned learn from this experience so that the organisation benefits and can apply the learning?

This final question is the one that can lead to the most value. All organisations these days have to be more innovative in response to the conditions at large: the fast-changing global marketplace, the political environment, emerging and unexpected competitors, more demanding consumers and more demanding employees. To my mind this small book about this small innovation experiment has a value way beyond its size. It is a valuable tool for anyone who is interested in delving into how on earth to create work cultures where people can experiment and innovate. This is the stuff that true learning is built from.

It is an accolade to Mike and the team that they took the risk to do this project. Aside from their own achievement and learning, they have given others the opportunity to learn too. That is a vulnerable situation to put yourself in and can feel extremely exposing. I take my hat off to them all.

Sally Bibb

Sally is a founding director of the performance consultancy talentsmoothie ltd. and award-winning author of books like: A Question of Trust (with Jeremy Kourdi), The Stone Age Company and Management f-Laws (with Russell Ackoff and Herbert Addison). She is also passionate about Argentine tango.

Reading Matter

Before starting, the team members were invited to read a number of books and articles. As Ludwig noted, almost no-one read all of them. But all of them had been read by someone. Let's see what the reading matter had to offer:

From *Sticky Wisdom* they had learnt that the six steps to starting something exciting in your company are ...

- **Freshness** – this is lateral-thinking, out-of-the-box stuff: find other ways to describe things, find analogies in other fields, challenge assumptions and make random connections.

- **Greenhousing** – stay in the SUN (Suspend judgement, Understand and Nurture), and keep out of the RAIN (don't React, Assume and INsist).

- **Realness** – make ideas real as soon as possible, don't try to be perfect, share prototypes.

- **Momentum** – manage energy and keep things going.

- **Signalling** – tell others how you want them to respond to your ideas – analytically, emotionally, supportively, critically...

- **Courage** – find it through positive self-commentary, getting support from friends, conviction, visualise how things could be.

The team followed a lot of this advice. They had SUN only sessions and reminded each other about signalling. Their coach, Javier, in particular, encouraged them to get out and talk to friends and to visualise the future, as part of managing the ebb and flow of energy in the group. Lack of time and becoming-whale-of-an-idea inhibited them when it came to making ideas real, though. If you're going to change the world you don't want to stuff up by missing an important clause in your Terms & Conditions.

But who knows? Reacting and Insisting might be really helpful in some teams. Being open to whatever kind of reaction you get from colleagues may open doors. Clear, analytical thinking is useful when making incremental change. And so on.

I like 'Signalling', though. And I saw it at work. Rather than the 'say three positive things first' approach or the 'criticise with abandon' Straw Man, it seems to me really helpful to signal the kind of feedback you're looking for. After all, who knows if the current idea is one you've been quietly working on for a couple of weeks or something you googled half-an-hour ago?

- - - - - -

In *Innovation: The Classic Traps*, Rosabeth Moss Kanter says that, after the dot-com crash, companies have focused on organic growth again. She concludes, however, that they shouldn't listen to current customers because it can inhibit 'breakthrough' innovation. Her classic traps include:

- Setting the hurdles too high or making the scope too narrow – not a problem for the Red Stripe team who had almost no constraints imposed on them.

- Making controls too tight – requiring innovations to meet conventional, commercial criteria. You could argue this one either way with Red Stripe. In the end, they were challenged by the GMC and their expert advisers on commercial grounds. They needn't have been if they had just 'gone for it', as they were allowed to do by their brief, but sooner or later they would have had to face the commercial music.

- Leadership too weak and communication too poor – these are traps for the organisation as a whole as much as for the innovation team. But she adds that 'top managers frequently put the best technical people in charge, not the best leaders'. These people 'emphasise tasks over relationships.' I discuss this in relation to Gerard Fairtlough's assertion that leadership is a task (See **Creative Compartments**, page 151). But managing relationships within the team is also a task. I talked to Joanna about this and she told me that she 'would have been more involved in discussing interpersonal issues openly... would have felt better about it if obvious permission had been given', even though she agreed that the team as a whole *had* given themselves permission to do that.

- Closed environments – Kanter maintains that 'by failing to tap others' ideas, [teams produce] lackluster recommendations; and by failing to keep peers informed, they [miss] getting buy-in... '. Neither was a problem for Red Stripe. But, in accepting Mike's conclusion that they perhaps went to the GMC too soon, and thus found themselves changing tack in response to the committee's objections, it's worth remembering Kanter's opposite warning that teams which work in secret and then present their ideas fully formed at the end may 'face unexpected objections that sometimes kill the project.'

- - - - - -

For Clayton Christensen, *The Innovator's Dilemma* is that, while listening to existing customers can inhibit innovation (because they don't necessarily know what they want or what's good for them), listening to existing customers can be the key to survival (because they sometimes know exactly what they want and what's good for them). The distinction has to do with sustaining and disruptive innovation and technologies. Customers are obviously better at imagining and wanting the former than the latter.

Additionally, organisations dominant in their sector, according to Christensen, tend to focus on maintaining the product and service quality that won them their customers in the first place. This leaves new entrants free to focus on developing new products, services or applications.

Because disruptive technologies are often serving entirely new markets, and because markets that do not exist cannot be analysed, established companies will tend to shy away from investing in them. Among the answers are setting up 'innovation islands' in large businesses, spinning off start-up groups, taking equity positions in (i.e. buying bits of) new, independent companies, and so on.

From this point of view, it looks like The Economist Group was doing the right thing when the GMC decided to stand back and give Project Red Stripe a free hand to implement whatever idea it chose without first seeking approval from Group management. But, in practice, as we've seen, this was an unrealistic decision. The management team needed to know if the Economist Group was about to be committed to an expensive, high-profile, not-for-profit venture.

In his book, Christensen describes at some length the innovation process in the computer hard drive manufacturing sector. He explains how it simply wasn't appropriate in 1979 for an established computer hard drive manufacturer to get out of the 8-inch drive business (where its customers were) and into the 5¼-inch drive business (which didn't yet exist). But the predictable result was that the established manufacturer was supplanted by a newcomer and eventually went bust. In the same way, it wouldn't have been appropriate for *The Economist* to focus on a philanthropy exchange website when its magazine publishing business was doing better then ever. One answer would have been to spin the idea off and invest in it if they liked the idea enough.

[Incidentally, I notice that the first of the SIPs (Statistically Improbable Phrases) that amazon.com lists for Christensen's book is 'value network framework'. Not only statistically, but also linguistically, improbable, I think.]

- - - - - -

The fourth book on the reading list that Mike gave the team at the outset was *The Power of the Tale*. The authors demonstrate pretty convincingly how story telling in business can build honesty and trust, promote learning, develop new skills, break new ground (or paths) and create scenarios that you can use in planning for the future.

For me, story telling is essentially a sales technique. It's a way of talking to, and winning over, the heart when the mind ain't listening. It's what Javier urged the team to do a lot more of, and something they focused on when creating an 'elevator pitch' and other justifications for their ideas. It's also part of the process of convincing yourself so you can convince others. Put like that, it sounds a tad mechanical. But then, what aspect of a relationship isn't, when you deconstruct it?

This business of story telling as a way of winning over others also reminds me of Georges Dumézil's assertion *in Mitra-Varuna* that sovereignty has two poles: the magician-king, who uses capture, bonds, knots, webs and nets, and the jurist-priest who governs by treaties, laws, pacts and contracts. The former, if I understand right, has more to do with feelings and intuition, the latter has more to do with analysis and logic. Officially, business is done on the basis of analysis and logic and run by jurist-priests; in practice, it is often run by magician-kings operating by capture and ensnarement. Story telling is a practice of ensnarement. And ensnarement and manipulation have managed to get themselves a bad name.

Julie Allan, one of the co-authors of *The Power of the Tale* is, I discover, currently working on, and researching, wisdom and its emergence in organisations. Interestingly, she quotes Walter Benjamin (who appears in **Drifting, Angst and Pan-ic**, page 29) thus:

> *"Counsel woven into the fabric of real life is wisdom,"*
> *writes author Walter Benjamin, reflecting on storytelling in*
> *Illuminations (1970). And, ". . . counsel is less an answer to a*
> *question than a proposal concerning the continuation of a*
> *story which is just unfolding."*

'Wisdom' seems to me a bold word to use. Sitting on top of the Systems Thinking hierarchy of data, information, knowledge, understanding, wisdom, it's a topic we've tended to leave to Solomon and the enlightened and I find it slightly shocking to see it discussed in day-to-day organisational terms. Editing the English translation of Alain de Vulpian's *Towards the Third Modernity* recently, I wanted to keep 'informed' as the translation of 'avisé'. The author wanted 'wise' and we compromised on 'wiser' because 'a wise organisation' seemed to me such an improbable creature. So wisdom seems like a fascinating object of study.

- - - - - -

Last on the list was Patty Seybold's *Outside Innovation*. I can't do better than quote the introduction:

> *What is Outside Innovation? It's when customers lead the design of your business processes, products, services, and business models. It's when customers roll up their sleeves to co-design their products and your business. It's when customers attract other customers to build a vital customer-centric ecosystem around your products and services.*

So she is addressing one part of the solution to the innovator's dilemma (above). And she makes an interesting point in the book, but more clearly in a recent blog, about predicting the future using crowdsourcing. Her blog points us to the Sloan Center for Internet Retailing's eLab eXchange prediction market. Red Stripe was not trying to predict the future using crowdsourcing but trying to get ideas about what it should do. One of the ideas it received related to setting up a prediction market (which it had already considered at length in the early days). So, by extension, something that Red Stripe *could* have done would have been to set up a prediction market for itself – getting people to bet on what would be the 'innovative and web-based product, service or business model' that it would come up with. Though it sounds improbable, the wisdom of crowds would perhaps have prevailed.

Dilemmas

- Don't react and insist, even though reacting and insisting may sometimes be really useful?

- Loosen controls… but not all of them and not too far.

- Look outside for the best ideas and share them early to get buy-in and avoid last-minute resistance, says Rosabeth Moss Kanter. But for the Project Red Stripe team, who did both assiduously, one lesson was perhaps that they looked outside too long and shared too early.

- Most organisations don't want to be disrupted. Yet many of the most significant innovations and innovation technologies have been definitively disruptive.

- Listening to existing customers can inhibit innovation and also be the key to survival.

- Story telling – in business as elsewhere – can build honesty and trust, but it is a practice of ensnarement and manipulation (or vocipulation. Why doesn't the word exist?).

- Can you use a prediction market to avoid making any decisions at all yourself?

===

Notes – Reading Matter

- *Sticky Wisdom* is [Allan, Dave et al., 2002]. Of all the books the team was asked to read, this was the one most often referred to.
- The Terms & Conditions set by the team for people submitting ideas (inevitably) received a lot of flak. You'll find links to both (T&Cs and flak) from the online edition.
- The straw man idea is covered in **The Straw Man,** of course (page 78).
- *Innovation: The Classic Traps* is [Kanter, 2006].
- Leadership as a task is discussed in **Creative Compartments,** page 151.
- *The Innovator's Dilemma* is [Christensen, 2000].
- *The Power of The Tale* is [Allan, Julie et al., 2002].
- *Mitra-Varuna* is [Dumézil, 1990].
- *Outside Innovation* is [Seybold, 2006].
- Patty Seybold's blog is Outside Innovation, listed in the **Blography.**
- Prediction markets are also mentioned in **Bright Ideas,** page 168.

The Practical Visionary

'The Practical Visionary' is the title of a *Strategy & Business* article published in 2008.

It's a good article, though curiously it offers a case study of the trajectory of the US National Basketball Association's CIO after his arrival at the organisation in 1999. Which is fine, except that the article is making a particular point about the role of the CIO *today*.

[Incidentally, I had to check whether 'The Power of TODAY' had become a business mantra to match The Power of Now in the realm of personal development. Google gave me prodigious results, but I had no energy to plough through the first 50 pages in order to find out the real number that it would eventually drop down to. I suspect that I had no energy because I'm not a vegan. Vegans run marathons where we carnos jog mere furlongs. I learnt this from the magnificent Steve Pavlina, who was No. 2 on Google's results list for 'The Power of TODAY'. No. 1 was a page at Microsoft.com. I don't think I've ever intentionally visited that site (though my computer probably visits regularly, especially late at night). Anyway, Steve's got a whole thing going about trying to change habits by deciding to do something for 30 days rather than for ever. Like giving up smoking or arms dealing or child abuse. (He doesn't say the latter two; they're my interpolation your honour.) He gave up meat first of all and then, feeling the onset of scorn for lacto-ovo vegetarians – and rightly so, in my opinion, as they betray a palpable lack of rigour – he gave up eggs and dairy products. As he goes on to tell us:

> *Well, I lost seven pounds in the first week, mostly from going to the bathroom as all the accumulated dairy mucus was cleansed from my bowels (now I know why cows need four stomachs to properly digest this stuff).*

Now I'm no farmer, but apart from suckling calves, I don't think I've ever seen a member of the cow family eating butter or cream or yoghurt or crème fraiche or any of that kind of mucus. They generate it, but tend not to ingest it. But perhaps Steve was 'avin' a laugh. No. No, he can't be. Because he goes on to tell us that,

> Recently I competed in Toastmasters International's annual humor speech contest... I won at the club level but lost the area contest. Technically I came in last place because I was disqualified for running over the time limit. If you go even one second overtime in these contests, you lose automatically.

Enough. Believe me, he wasn't 'avin' a larf.]

Back to the practical visionary. As Michael Farber and his co-authors tell us,

> the model 21st-century CIO... is training his focus on the demand side of the IT business equation, where the needs of the business are paramount, rather than spending most of his time on such typical supply-side concerns as cutting IT costs...

In case it's not immediately obvious, that means that he or she is getting involved with planning the corporate strategy and helping to deliver it, rather than spending too much time worrying about whether people's PCs work or the intranet's secure. (Of course, those things still matter but, in this case, the guy had several years from 1999 onwards to fix them before moving on to strategy.)

They go on:

> The strategic CIO has never been more important to the future of the organisation. As operations and markets become more fragmented, there is an ever-greater need for IT to bind together a company and augment its collective intellect... IT can be used to address problems of mounting complexity and to help an organisation move into new products, new processes, and new markets, at home and around the world. New technologies are always changing how companies operate internally and how they look at their customers, suppliers, partners, sales channels, and markets.

Remember that Mike was CIO at The Economist Group, where he was doing exactly that – rolling up his sleeves and getting involved on the innovation front line.

Reading on, the article could have been written about Red Stripe:

> The new CIO has an opportunity to change the way organisations adopt and use technology. Moreover, the time for changing it has never been better. The range of Web 2.0 technologies – social networking software, video-sharing sites, multi-participant simulated environments, and creative exchanges has sparked a level of excitement not seen since the early days of the Internet.

Isn't that what we've just been saying? I'll keep quoting:

> CIOs should study all the new technologies coming down the pipeline, whether or not they appear to be suited to the CIO's company or industry. CIOs need to take the time to think about their potential strategic value, not today, but five or 10 years from now. And they should talk with their peers within the company about how such technologies might fit in with strategies they too are seeing down the road. If CIOs aren't keeping these emerging technologies on their radar, it is at their peril: they can bet there's a competitor out there who is.

In all these respects, the six months that Mike and his team spent on Project Red Stripe seem to have been right on target. They were even talking explicitly about developing an idea that would reflect where the Group should be in 5-10 years in terms of its Internet presence. And any one of the team could brief the Group on where and how to look to find out what's over the horizon.

So, we come back to the perception thing. Though I haven't witnessed this for myself first hand, my sense from the recent silence about Red Stripe at The Economist Group is that it's not seen as a success. Yet, in an odd way, I think the way it turned out could be one of the best outcomes for the Group.

For example, far from being surprised by the Financial Times's move into offering high priced (c. £2,000 p.a.) social networking sites for its executive readers in areas like Media & Technology, Property and the 'Luxury Sector' in February 2008, The Economist Group knew all about the pros and cons and had in-depth research on the idea at its fingertips.

Equally, from early 2008, changes at the Economist.com website inevitably began to reflect some of the possibilities previously discussed by the Red Stripe team and rejected as 'too incremental'. Now, of course, some of these might have happened anyway, but the team regularly invited *Economist* executives into their room to share their thoughts, which were also shared more widely on the team's blog. And Mike and other members of the team who have stayed with the company are available to discuss their inside knowledge of everything from starting a predictions market to 'intelligent product placement' to an open-authoring wiki.

Dilemmas:

- If you give smart employees the opportunity of a lifetime, how do you hang on to them once the excitement's over? [For once, there's an answer to this one. Help them to move on, if that's what they need to do. Stay in touch. Maybe they'll come back even more fully fledged.]

Notes – The Practical Visionary

- The *Strategy & Business* article is [Farber et al., 2008].
- Steve Pavlina's website is at www.stevepavlina.com
- *The Power of Now* is [Tolle, 1999]. Only Simon Curle could have persuaded me to read this book, which changed my life, though I still wince when admitting it.
- The *Financial Times* forums can be found at www.ftexecutiveforums. com
- Prediction markets, intelligent product placement and other ideas are discussed at greater length in **Bright Ideas**, page 168.

Thunderbirds are go

Stewart: *'We were going to decorate the room ourselves but we couldn't be bothered.'*

7th February 2007

The room is almost square. White. With an alcove for filing drawers and two stacking boxes that don't stack. They stand lopsided, empty.

Two tables are pushed together to make one and stand against the wall where the window is. The window goes from floor to ceiling, with a white blind pulled half way down. On the opposite wall is a large white screen showing the contents of Stewart's laptop screen.

In the far corner is a white spiral staircase going heavenward. Coats hang from the staircase. To begin with the team can retreat in ones and twos up the staircase to another meeting room but, later, this is reappropriated by the agency.

There is just about room to walk round the tables when people are sitting down without asking them to pull their chairs in. On the tables are six laptops (occasionally more), later on most with a separate mouse and full-size keyboard in front of them and, later on still, most propped up on silver laptop stands. A tangle of cables and leads run over the tables and down through round holes to an extension socket on the floor. Morning and evening consist of the ritual plugging and unplugging of these leads and accessories and some scrabbling on the floor.

Each team member has a separate locking drawer in which they can leave their valuables and (if necessary) their laptop. Later this system fails when Ludwig locks his drawer without realising that Tom's laptop is in it and leaves for a long weekend in Berlin. It fails again when Steven loses his key and has to force the drawer. Some unhappiness ensues on each occasion.

At the same end of the room as the door the webcam offers a soundless, always-on vision of the room and its contents. On my computer at home, where I check the webcam periodically to see if a fight or other act of unexpected intimacy has erupted, the picture updates approximately twice a second with the result that the team members move with the same supermarionated rhythm as the cast of Thunderbirds.

By mid-February the room has assumed a slightly different configuration and will more or less stay this way until the end. The tables are now pushed into the centre of the room, so people can sit on all four sides of the oblong that they create. The blind tends to be up and, as summer approaches, the window is usually open. The screen has been raised and there are now two whiteboards on the wall, which are occasionally covered in idea clouds, target dates and to-do lists. On February it had a list showing everyone's mobile phone number. Intuitively, that didn't seem like the easiest way to communicate the information. On reflection, it probably was.

The door to the room slams shut whenever someone enters or leaves the office. The room shudders slightly and everyone is jolted. By the time of my last visit in July the team are perfecting a device invented by Joanna. It involves folding a piece of cardboard and inserting it into the gap between the door frame and the hinged side of the door, which serves to slow down the speed with which the door closes and reduce the slam to a gentle pffftt.

Wall decorations are almost non-existent. One or two pieces of fruit and a packet of biscuits occasionally decorate the centre of the table. There is no other concession to homeliness.

The drone of central London traffic (average daytime traffic speed 6.1 mph/9.76 kph), punctuated by the wail of regular post-war-on-terror-and-current-war-on-gun-crime sirens, intrudes, as does the squeal and hiss of air brakes. Otherwise the outside world is largely excluded.

As Richard Ogle and many others have observed, this kind of insulation isn't obviously the best way to foster innovation:

> If you don't experience the problem you are solving, you are unlikely to solve it in an innovative way.

> Locking six people up in a room for six months with £100,000 isn't giving them much of an opportunity to experience problems.

And again:

> ... cognitive scientists, researchers in artificial intelligence, psychologists, and philosophers have begun to talk about how the mind extends out into the world. This revolutionary expansion of the traditional concept of mind directly challenges our belief in the individual mind's internal self-sufficiency.

> We are coming to understand that in making sense of the world, acting intelligently, and solving problems creatively, we do not rely solely on our mind's internal resources. Instead, we constantly have recourse to a vast array of culturally and socially embodied idea-spaces that populate the extended mind. These spaces – manifested in forms as various as myths, business models, scientific paradigms, social conventions, practices, institutions, and even computer chips – are rich with embedded intelligence that we have progressively offloaded into our physical, social, and cultural environment for the sake of simplifying the burden on our own minds of rendering the world intelligible. Sometimes the space of ideas thinks for us. We live in a smart world.

That said, there's the small question of those six eyes on the world provided by the team's propped-up laptops. We tend to forget, even though we chant the truism as a mantra, that the Internet has changed the way we see the world. Six people checking the blogs of some of the cleverest minds on the planet, inviting the bright ideas of many more, reading and researching as they go, saving and sharing their discoveries via Delicious and, eventually and inevitably, having lunch with their would-be clients and users are less insulated in many ways than any human beings at any time in history.

On the other hand, Sandra Reeve observes how, in the way we move, we are shaped by our environment, the people in it and our experience of it (I walk like my parents and I walk appropriately –

differently, for example, if I grew up on a hill or if I'm in the habit of moving through dangerous places). She reminds us that our preoccupation with how we can change our environment conceals the extent to which it changes us. And this is no less true of our ways of thinking about organisations, change, work and innovation.

Incidentally, they also had the fine minds of Abbott Mead Vickers BBDO (who had lent them their office) along the corridor. In February the team had watched the new BBC2 idents (designed by the agency and launched that month) and Steven had told me that there were plenty of people in the agency who could be very useful to them. Though they used Clare Hutchinson, one of the agency's account planners, to facilitate an early brainstorming session, they didn't otherwise draw on this resource.

The World Wide Web is an idea-space *par excellence,* though it's perhaps less effective as a mind-space. Most of the team members felt they thought more widely and creatively when they were out of the office and an ideas session in Regent's Park was often quoted as a particular instantiation of that. Mike said in March, 'We need to do something that gets people into a different place. I mean out of the office; where we can be creative.' At the same time Steven said 'Yes, everyone agrees that this room is pretty dingy. We're going to try and get out into the park more once the weather's better.' But, once the weather got better, there was never really time. So they didn't.

Moving around does seem like a good idea. And/or working in a balmier climate, where you can be outside more. There's even some science behind this now. Nicholas Humphrey asserts that, 'sensations are not things that happen *to us,* they are things *we do*'. So sensation 'is on the production side of the brain rather than the reception side'. Clearly, having good ideas also occurs on the 'production side'. If this means anything, and it may not, it means that our thinking is more likely to be closely involved with what we are sensing than one might at first imagine. In which case, we perhaps need to be aware of environmental changes that lead to us sensing differently – or *doing* different sensations – so that we can encourage ourselves to *do* different thoughts.

Worried by their feeling stuck, partly because they were constantly together in the same room, Javier (who observes that, 'when stuck, teams go into intellectualising mode') had invited two of them to go away and come up with ideas for how the team should work for the next four months – practical ideas about where to work, how and when. 'Can I suggest you actually propose a solution, not just present ideas to talk about?', Javier had said. So Tom and Ludwig had come back with a 'Fresh Air Straw Man':

Intentions:

- *create a planning system which allows the team to work efficiently without having to be in the same room*
- *in other words: make sure that team "explodes" when it doesn't need to be together*

Promises:

- *have no more than 4 people in the office, except on "decision days"*
- *don't work from own home all three non-decision days*
- *try to work in other team members' home spaces*
- *try not to be offline for more than half an hour*
- *try to work in more inspirational places*

Actions:

- *clear this with group*
- *purchase head sets and web cams for all of us*
- *identify spaces to work in (Starbucks, museums, homes, parks with wifi coverage, etc...)*
- *find a good online planning tool*
- *get smaller desks and re-arrange the room*
- *organise trip to Berlin*

They discussed the Straw Man but couldn't reach any agreement on a new way of working, so things carried on as before. Their internal blog said just: 'We disagreed on how to work.'

Dilemmas:

- Stay in or go out? Of course, the street, the park, the café all offer different perspectives. But are these necessarily more conducive to innovation than the perspectives offered by a dozen good blogs or websites?

- Stay together or move apart? Absence, as we know, makes the heart grow fonder. Or less irritated. How important is it to be able to communicate instantly all the time?

- Prioritise intellect or prioritise context/ecology? Where do good ideas start? Some, of course, are carefully reasoned, while others appear to arrive unbidden. What context best affords intuitive insight? If the answer is different for different team members, who gets to decide?

- Zoom in or zoom out?

- If the answer is always 'both', how do you decide when to do which? (**See Rules and Values**, page 114.)

Notes – Thunderbirds are Go

- There are pictures (albeit grainy) of the office in the online book.
- The people at Midas Oracle had submitted an idea about prediction markets. They thought it was a very good idea. After discovering that Red Stripe were unlikely to adopt it they became petulant and on 26th March posted a shot from the webcam showing Stewart reading the paper and Steven drinking coffee a tad dreamily.

  Then two days later, the people at Midas Oracle posted a camgrab, again from the Red Stripe webcam, purporting to show Stewart reading the previous Midas Oracle blog post, which referred to him reading the paper and Steven drinking coffee. 'Snake,' as they rightly said, 'eats itself'.
- On experiencing problems, see [Ogle, 2007].
- The 'locking six people up in a room' quote is from Suw Charman-Anderson's blog listed under Strange.Corante in the **Biography**. The longer quote is from [Ogle, 2007].
- On Nicholas Humphrey, see [Humphrey, 2006].
- The Straw Man idea is explained, appositely enough, in **The Straw Man**, page 78.
- On movement, environment and context, see [Reeve, 2008].

Creative Compartments

Tom: *'I call him Ludwig* [said with a w not a v] *because he says Vikipedia.'*

Even though it's not, strictly-speaking, relevant because the 'compartments' he talks about are much larger than the six-pack at Project Red Stripe, I want to refer to the late Gerard Fairtlough's book *Creative Compartments* because Gerard talked to the team early in February and they made their first presentation to him at Northcote House. Although his role was far less significant than Javier's, he was an important influence at the start for some team members who said they felt able to 'take ourselves seriously' as the result of the former head of Shell Chemicals and Celltech calling in to visit them.

Gerard's prescription for facilitating an 'explosion of innovation' includes a range of features. Some of the features relevant here are:

Alignment of personal and group goals – there should be a good overlap between the goals and values of individuals and those of the group as a whole, but not so much overlap that variety vanishes.

In **On Experts and Expertise** (see page 202), I talk about the variety of skills that the team members brought to the project and that's probably the natural starting point for thinking about a team when you're selecting its members. But, of course, from the inside, goals and values are far more likely to inform the day-to-day business of working together. Gerard quotes Roberto Unger quoting Goethe: 'against the superior gifts of another person there is no defence but love' and says that the political or organisational equivalent is strong sympathy. Strong sympathy is an easy thing to say; it can be imagined or feigned or supposed (in the absence of overt criticism); but it's hard to sustain when our habit as humans is mostly to leap to judgement and criticism of the other, the different. Though the team clearly shared a vision of success for the project, and though they shared a self-interest in a good outcome in personal career terms, they had sharply differing views, at times, of how that outcome was to be achieved. Most important, their shared vision of success did not include a shared view of what they could hope to achieve. One person's 'let's change the world' was another team member's 'pie in the sky'.

Structure in decision-making – Gerard draws attention to the fact that a lack of structure in decision-making can lead to unending debate and threaten effectiveness and fairness. We've seen in **The Straw Man** (page 78) the problems caused at times by exactly this issue and the fruitful resolution of some of those problems with techniques like the straw man and the one-minute meeting (which was exactly that – an opportunity to reach quick decisions on issues without embarking on a lengthy opinion-sharing process)...

Rotation and distribution of tasks – the rotation of tasks within a group spreads understanding of task variety and reduces complacency. Again, I've described in **Maps** (page 35) how the team moved quickly from, for example, Ludwig being the appointed scribe and blogger to sharing this and many other tasks although, inevitably again, some tasks are clearly dependent on established expertise. Stewart, for example, was always likely to be the one charged with website development. Gerard acknowledges this when he says, 'A little bit of specialisation may be sensible' and adds, when talking about the rotation of leadership, that 'perhaps not everyone wants to take the lead'.

An important additional point that he made when we discussed this is that 'leadership is a task'. It's all too easy for the tasks and roles to be allocated only after the structure and appropriate 'archy' of the team are in place, whereas it may be useful to consider team leadership as a task like any other.

Unconstrained communication – Gerard describes unconstrained communication as 'communication undistorted by the influence of power' and I think the exchanges reported in this book suggest that power and deference were not issues that unduly troubled the team. The constraint of tact, which he says is 'generally harmless' was sometimes an issue, as was, crucially, the constraint of time. Often people didn't say everything on their minds, feeling that further discussion of the objective would inhibit the team from achieving <u>any</u> objective. In this they were both right and wrong.

They could have talked around their becoming-whale-of-an-idea for the whole six months and not achieved the desired outcome, but the sharp change of tack in the final weeks of the project as they discovered that **Lughenjo** was not the right idea after all meant that this happened anyway.

When I discussed with Gerard the problems caused by the constraint of tact (which were perhaps exacerbated by the multicultural – though largely Anglo-Saxon – make-up of the team), he proposed a simple solution: post-meeting reviews. If every significant meeting were followed, he suggested, by a task review (what did we achieve?) and a process review (how did we do it?), it would have allowed room for an open airing of feelings that one team member had not spoken or contributed, that another had talked too much and without having any apparent point to make, or that a third had remained stubbornly wedded to a particular idea without acknowledging the possibility of alternatives.

While there often wasn't time for such meetings, I did witness some at Marylebone Road where precisely such discussions were had, but they tended to be done as people were packing up for the day or going to lunch or making coffee. They tended also to be a time for one person to recapitulate – having just concluded a meeting people often didn't want to embark on another. (Interestingly, when I talked to Mike about this, he observed that some of the most important conversations were had at the end of the day as people were leaving. Of course, it *is* a time when people may want to 'off-load' concerns or seek reassurance, rather than taking a problem home. Equally, it is often also a time when some people are absent or not fully focused on the question. As in marriage and psychotherapy, some of the most important things are said in 'door-handle conversations' just as one person is leaving.)

Communicating about facts, ethics and feelings – closely related to the previous point, Fairtlough stresses the importance of trust in open communication about facts, ethics and feelings. He also reminds us that the three issues need to be approached and handled differently.

In **Rules and Values** (page 114) I describe how the team early on identified the need for openness, tolerance and loyalty (and, in fact, gave these priority over other more mechanical or practical virtues like hard work or punctuality). So there was no lack of awareness of the importance of these virtues (for example, as Fairtlough puts it, of knowing how and when to say, 'it doesn't sound to me as if you really mean that'). What perhaps was lacking was the time to apply those virtues.

Dissent for the sake of task – Fairtlough argues that individuals in any team must be prepared to disagree for the sake of the task in hand: 'In most businesses, there is disagreement about the future.' This was certainly true at Project Red Stripe and must be true, almost by definition, of any innovation project. In guessing about the future, everyone draws on their past experience and judgements.

Most established business organisations are strongly contained, shaped and influenced by what they have done, sold or been good at in the past. To survive into the future they have to innovate constantly. Their employees, working in the present, are sandwiched between the weight of the past (including their own personal experiences, successes and failures) and the possibilities of the future (including their own ambitions, dreams and fears).

As Gerard Fairtlough rightly observes, 'If a group of people is capable of communicating about these different judgements, and of synthesising them into something better than any of them, then the group has an enormously valuable resource.'

My experience at Red Stripe was that the team could really motor when it managed to do this, and could be held back when it didn't. And I was reminded of an approach to argument that I was first introduced to by Theodore Zeldin: namely, that the participants in an argument should rather spend time helping their antagonists refine and improve their stated position than devote themselves to belittling those rival positions and asserting the merits of their own.

New mental models – summarising his recipe for delivering change via creative compartments, Gerard Fairtlough refers to the work of Don

Michael, who reminds us that unfamiliar situations, ambiguous roles and not knowing answers can provoke in us denial and resistance and a desire to hand over responsibility to a strong leader. This is as true of a work team, an organisation or a nation. Part of the solution he proposes is the building of new mental models. And one way of doing that is through story telling. Then a novelty in business, but now less so, stories are a way of linking past, present and future, of setting out our values, of achieving a harmonious approach without sinking into 'groupthink'.

Fairtlough refers to the story of progress and modernisation, to the 'green story' and to what Don Michael and Walter Anderson have called the 'new paradigm' story. This is the story of, and belief in, 'super-progress: a sudden leap forward to an entirely new way of being and a new way of understanding the world'. I don't think it's too trite to relate this idea of the new paradigm story to Red Stripe's hunt for the becoming-whale-of-an-idea. Perhaps their experience as a team will help to provide a story for future innovation teams.

Dilemmas:

- In the long run, is it wiser to prioritise skills or goals and values when forming a team? And, whichever you choose, at what point does diversity cease to be productively provocative and become unproductively divisive?

- Does it matter that a team shares a vision of success if its members don't share a sense of how likely it is that success can be achieved?

- For some people, it may be more important to arrive at the wrong decision fairly than to reach the right decision unfairly or undemocratically. This can be an important constraint on the likelihood of achieving a successful outcome in anything.

- Should the role of leader be allocated like any other task, or handled separately and first?

- If some of the most important team conversations are had at moments when not everybody is present or paying attention (and they are), how do you create a structure that allows those conversations to be heard, managed and recorded without destroying the less formal situations that allow the conversations to take place?

- Unfamiliar situations, ambiguous roles and not knowing answers (characteristics of any successful innovation project) can provoke in us denial and resistance and a desire to hand over responsibility to a strong leader (characteristics of any unsuccessful innovation project).

Notes – Creative Compartments

- The quotes are all from [Fairtlough, 1994].
- Fairtlough is at pains to credit Jurgen Habermas [1981] with developing the theory of unconstrained communication.
- In *Creative Compartments* and at his talk to the Society for Organisational Learning in 2007, Fairtlough credited Jane Jacobs for the term 'dissent for the sake of task' and the thinking behind it. [Jacobs, 1992].
- Theodore Zeldin's wonderful book on conversation is [Zeldin, 1998].
- On new mental models, see [Michael, 1973] and [Michael & Anderson, 1989]. Incidentally, Don Michael and Walter Truett Anderson were talking about the way in which different interest groups were co-opting the problem of global warming for their own ends in the late 1980s – twenty years later, their arguments are still provocative and radically incisive.
- On the role of story telling in business, see [Allan et al., 2002].

Web 2.0

Stewart (after searching for an easy way to time people's contributions in a meeting): *'There's an online stopwatch. That's fantastic.'*

Tom (with reference to the number of ideas that had been coming in about social networking and Web 2.0): *'Can you see other people's stopwatches? Are there other times that people have chosen. Like 5 minutes. 10 minutes?'*

On one visit to Red Stripe, I was struck by the amount of talk about Web 2.0 that I had heard – and by how little I knew about it. (Social networking, mash-ups, things like that.) But what precisely did the term Web 2.0 mean? [The received pronunciation in the UK seems to be 'two point nought'. In the USA it's 'two point oh'. In the UK we're also allowed to say 'two zero' or 'two point zero'. In French it's 'deux point zéro' and in German 'zwei-punkt-null'. There, now some of us can talk more confidently at parties.]

To assuage my conscience I read a long piece on Web 2.0 by Tim O'Reilly, who more or less invented the term. (And, in writing this, I've also had to learn about Web 3.0, which Eric Schmidt defines better than I can. O'Reilly – who wrote his piece in September 2005, so it's out of date, but still seems sensible to me – identifies a number of key differentiators between first- and second-generation Internet successes, Web 1.0 and 2.0 respectively. Since Red Stripe was developing a second-generation Internet presence for *The Economist*, I'm going to look at some of these differentiators here. This is as technical as the book is going to get, so please don't be put off or over-excited, depending on your orientation:

Web 1.0 – Publishing ~ Web 2.0 – Participation

This looks, on the face of it, to be the key differentiator for a publisher like *The Economist*, whose business has been built on the quality of the proprietary information that it gathers and publishes. In Web 2.0 models, user participation is the key – Wikipedia vs. Britannica Online, for example. This initially looked alarming for the project, except that *Economist* readers are highly intelligent, well-informed people [Q. What might Wikipedia look like if its contributors were exclusively *Economist* readers? A. Well, better in parts. Its coverage of the OECD or trading in carbon emissions might be more extensive, informative and hotly debated, while its coverage of hip-hop or ramming speed computer games would probably be thin.]

The key phrase in all this is probably 'hotly debated'. The conversation that would take place between all *Economist* readers would be potentially riveting (for other *Economist* readers). But, as the article also identifies, user-participation is a rather too simplistic model: 'only a small percentage of users will go to the trouble of adding value to your application'. Therefore, you should set inclusive defaults for aggregating user data as a side effect of their use of the application. In other words, knowing what other *Economist* readers think is useful. But limited. Knowing what other websites they use would be potentially more useful.

Other attributes:

Web 1.0 – All rights reserved ~ Web 2.0 – Some rights reserved

What can Red Stripe achieve by syndicating, disseminating or letting go of copyright control of its content with a view to getting more people to visit its site?

Web 1.0 – Serving the head ~ Web 2.0 Serving the long tail

Where *The Economist*'s print products have to deliver as many articles as possible of maximum interest to its core readership, *Economist 2.0* has to find ways also to serve exceptional readers with outlandish or niche interests.

Web 1.0 – Static sites ~ Web 2.0 – Dynamic sites

How can *Economist 2.0* deliver a database-backed site with dynamically generated content that matches the individual user's needs?

Web 1.0 – Control ~ Web 2.0 – Co-operate

Web 2.0 services (and they're services, not platforms or products) are built of a network of co-operating services. Therefore: offer web services interfaces and content syndication, and re-use the data services of others. Support lightweight programming models that allow for loosely coupled systems.

So, Project Red Stripe always had to do something at least 2.0, but it also had to avoid the temptation to do it for the sake of it.

Notes – Web 2.0

- The online stopwatch is at http://tools.arantius.com/stopwatch
- Tim O'Reilly's thoughts are to be found at [O'Reilly, 2005] and Eric Schmidt's definition can be seen on YouTube at http://www.youtube.com/watch?v=T0QJmmdw3bo
- Apparently it's not necessarily true that only a small percentage of users will add value to your application. According to an alarming report from Universal McCann called 'When Did we Start Trusting Strangers?', in 10 out of 22 categories surveyed (including music, film, books and groceries), more people contribute online advice and opinion on products than seek the advice and opinion of others. Which, of course, is the underlying problem with the blog explosion: more people write them than read them.

Peter Drucker (and Gary Hamel)

I know you won't take me seriously unless I at least mention Peter Drucker. So here he comes.

In *Innovation and Entrepreneurship* he looked at the seven sources of innovation (there would be seven, wouldn't there? I bet he thought of six and then spent a week kicking his dog till he came up with the seventh.)

Want to know what they are?

Here they are anyway:

- Unexpected occurrences (in your industry/organisation) – to include unexpected successes and failures, as well as outside events.

- Gaps between perceptions in your industry/organisation and reality – these may be gaps between what <u>your customers</u> think you do/ behave like/make money from and what <u>you</u> think you do/behave like/make money from, or gaps between what the media says and the reality from the inside.

- Process weaknesses or needs – you may know these or your customers may be able to tell you.

- Industry and market changes – including new technology, new competitors, changing economic realities, etc.

- Demographic changes – including ageing, birth, marriage and death patterns, changes to the social fabric and class system, changing patterns of wealth and ownership, urbanisation and cultural changes.

- Changes in customer attitudes and priorities.

- New technology and new scientific and business knowledge.

This is a good list. We nod at them knowingly. They're written in plain English. No wonder Drucker is a god. What he then tells you to do is also fairly simple. You gather a lot of data about all these things and you look at them. He has rules for looking at them. Nine rules, which is OK. Seven would have been better, but eight is a no-no. When you've done that, you consider the data, the opportunities and your ideas. First you consider them conceptually. That is, you think about them. Then you consider them perceptually. That is you talk to your customers and others who will be affected or involved.

Of course, it's not quite as simple as that, but it nearly is.

Peter Drucker's approach is confirmed by Dave Pollard, a prolific and insightful writer, who came up with a number of principles about the innovation process. The two most relevant to this discussion are:

- **Need Drives Innovation:** *Necessity is the mother of invention and... the important innovations and technologies of human history have addressed the greatest human needs of their age. Without an urgent human need, a burning platform, a Business Case, there will be no innovation...*

- **Innovation Starts with the Customer:** *If successful innovations must address an urgent human need, then the front-end of the innovation process should be situated at the point of contact with the humans expressing that need, i.e. the sales and customer service people in businesses, not the R&D laboratory or the marketing department. With some notable exceptions where the need for the innovation was only identified later, innovations coming from R&D tend to be solutions in search of problems, and those coming from Marketing tend to be solutions for which needs need to be artificially created through advertising.*

Now Red Stripe didn't do it the way Drucker and Pollard say they should have. They didn't, largely, I think, because these rules seem like a recipe for incremental change, when they were trying to make a conceptual leap. But I do wonder whether this approach might have got them to the same destination faster and more reliably and with more of the data that they needed for the business plan. Who knows? And if they didn't have God on their side in the form of Peter Drucker, then they had another: Gary Hamel. Hamel's recipe for innovation on a shoestring has four key ingredients, of which two are:

> **Use outside innovators.** *Use the Web to find people whose passions match your problems.*

And

> **Invest in the most radical ideas.** *For the biggest payoffs, avoid retreads, updates, or add-ons in favor of truly original concepts.*

One thing's for sure. Looking at customer perceptions, attitudes and priorities (which they didn't do because they weren't sure that they wanted to develop a product/service for their existing customers – maybe they would want to go after children, or women or the Third World) would have led them to frame their idea-gathering more along the lines of 'what do you want?' and less along the lines of 'what do you think we should do?'

That might seem like an unimportant distinction when customers are famous for not knowing what they want and for answering questions the way they think you want them to (and which is why more and more companies use corporate anthropologists to go and see what people really need but haven't yet realised they need). But I think it would have got them different answers. And since, in the end, they decided to try and service their existing customer base, it would have been an interesting approach.

While we're on recipes for innovation, Andrew Hargadon has got another one. And why wouldn't he have? After all, he's an Associate Professor of Technology Management at the Graduate School of Management at University of California, Davis, and Director of Technology Management programs there. Hargadon doesn't like the 'Great Man' theory of invention and comes close to saying that 'there's nothing new under the sun'.

Allowing that innovation, nonetheless, takes place, he stresses the importance of continuity. By recombining existing ideas – rather than inventing new ones – he suggests that we can better exploit the sources of innovation and increase their chances. To do this, he espouses 'technology brokering strategies' to help people move between different worlds, to see how ideas from one market's past can be used in new ways in another market.

So Hargadon's recipe is:

The future is already here – Find somebody who's doing something interesting and imagine where you can use it again. This is a different approach from the 'let's have an idea' one. It turns innovation into a search process, though a rather different search process from Project Red Stripe's whale hunt.

Analogy trumps invention – It's much easier to recognise the similarities between two things (analogy) rather than come up with something that you've never thought of.

Find your *discomfort* zone – The problem with being comfortable is that we tend to play our role appropriately and competently. It's difficult to try new things and think new thoughts. We're uncomfortable working in new settings, where we're unsure what's the right thing to do or the appropriate way to behave, and we're not sure that we have anything to contribute.

Divided we innovate – Keeping people divided allows them to go in different directions, which creates the variance you need later to find new combinations.

Rules 1 and 2 are a useful counter to the 'let's not be incremental' approach. Rule 3 is consolation for those who think they perhaps don't know enough to be on an innovation team. Rule 4 offers some comfort if you can't decide and are forced to pursue two or more ideas for a while.

This chapter might be starting to sound like, 'You should have done it this way Red Stripe'. It's not meant to. There are good arguments for avoiding the incremental, for not unsettling people, for working co-operatively not competitively. They're dotted around this book.

One thing's for sure. However you run an innovation project, a lot of people will gather round to tell you that you should have done it differently.

Dilemmas:

- As discussed throughout this book, there are sound reasons for turning to customers when looking for workable innovations, and sound reasons for avoiding their 'blinkered thinking'. Looking inside and outside the organisation both work. All innovation is, to some extent, incremental, but the most exciting innovations don't <u>feel</u> incremental. Keeping people divided can be fruitful or destructive. Actually, there are no rules that work all the time. And, if there were rules that worked all the time for innovation teams, it would instantly be innovative to break them.

Notes – Peter Drucker (and Gary Hamel)

- *Innovation and Entrepreneurship* is [Drucker, 1985].
- Dave Pollard's blog is listed as **How to Save the World** in the **Biography**. As always, see the online version of this book for the link to the post quoted here.
- On Gary Hamel's thinking in this context, see [Hamel & Getz, 2004].
- There's more on this whole question of whether or not to listen to customers when you're looking for innovations in the chapter on Clayton Christensen in **Reading Matter** (page 134).
- The 'Great Man' theory of innovation is close to Schumpeter's *unternehmergeist* – discussed in **Equifinality** (page 79).
- On Andrew Hargadon's recipe, see [Hargadon, 2003].

Alexander Bain and the Fax Machine

Stewart (writing to the agency they were hoping to use on **Lughenjo**): *'I'm trying to get a discount here. If they're called Reading Room now, imagine what they could be called if this goes well: Reading Hall, Reading Castle...'*

Joanna: *'Library?'*

At the time of writing, Stewart has never sent a fax in his life. At least he has never sent a fax using a fax machine.

I remember the first fax I sent. It was 1983, towards the end of the Golden Age of secretaries but before administrators had been invented. The fax machine lived in a distant office (it served three companies and an entire building) and was watched over by the cruel, but beautiful, fax empress. The empress reputedly observed with searing contempt one's bungled efforts to feed a sheet of paper the right way up into its electronic maw and then try to extract it again in order to read the recipient's fax number. It was not possible to ask the empress to send the fax for me as she was not my secretary. She didn't even work for the same company as me. Moreover, it was that watershed time in the social politics of feminism when, if you were a man wishing not to repeat the sins of his forefathers, asking a woman at work to do almost anything was problematic. More importantly, I was young and shy. In the end, I crept in during lunch and used the machine.

I sent my last fax in 2005. In 22 years, an entire communication technology was born, grew up, withered and died. The man who sold me my first fax machine now sells sustainable energy solutions for your home (formerly known as double glazing). I use my fax machine as a shelf for my wireless router. In much the same way as I grow strawberries in a cast out, cast iron bath in the garden. Office equipment magazines can no longer fill space with articles beginning with one of the most over-reported factoids of all time: namely, that the fax machine was invented in 1843.

In any case, Stew had never sent a fax. I watched him spend about 35 minutes working out how to configure the built-in modem on his laptop so that he could send the fax straight from his computer without first printing it. The fax related to the agreement he had reached with the website design agency. As he became increasingly frustrated with the technology, so his exasperation with the agency mounted. He asked with growing urgency what possible difference it could make whether he sent the electronically generated and electronically signed letter by fax or by email. Having completed the configuration, he spent a further ten minutes trying to get a dial tone. That done we were treated to the sound of the recipient machine ringing remorselessly. Stew finally declared, 'There is no answer'. Like that. He didn't say, 'There's no answer'; he said it as four words. Entering the office to hear the final minutes of the struggle, Mike finally said in a flat tone, 'There's a fax machine outside'. Stewart replied, 'There may be a fax machine outside'.

Somehow the challenge of cracking the old technology was as interesting to him as the challenge of cracking the new. Like all technology problems, it was a dragon, to be slain. The existence of a ready-made solution in the next room was entirely irrelevant. I suspect that everyone in the room knew that efficiency was not the point. An hour spent on (not) sending a fax was the very acceptable price of a problem-solving mindset which, in most other situations, was a priceless asset to the team as Stewart identified quick and cheap solutions to thorny programming difficulties in the final weeks.

Dilemmas:

- Half the population knows, almost from birth, that efficiency (like health) is very dull. How do you get people whose sense of self-esteem is based on chaos and inefficiency to be ordered and efficient?

Notes – Alexander Bain and the Fax Machine

- I learnt from Frank Price [1990] about the takiti and the golooma – two
  representations of two world views that, broadly speaking, look like
  chaos and order. But looking again at the book, I find he got the idea
  from another book (whose title he couldn't remember). Frank is a
  wonderful writer. Here's how he ends his section on the subject:

  > There is nothing 'right' nor anything 'wrong' about which of these
  > worlds you would choose as your abode, there is only your choice,
  > and anything that the choosing says about you it says to you alone;
  > that is all, and that is enough. You have chosen your world. You
  > chose it long ago, a long time before you picked out the takiti or the
  > golooma.

Bright ideas

I said I would write not about the content, but about the process. But I thought it might be interesting to take a quick look at what's going on at the bleeding edge of media and publishing, in relation to Project Red Stripe.

As I write, the ten most recent 'entrepreneurial ideas' listed in the Media & Publishing section of trend-spotting website springwise.com are:

1. A video-sharing website for skateboarders and surfers

2. A scheme to allow fans to fund their favourite singers or bands

3. Yideoz – a video-sharing site for the Jewish community

4. A content-sharing scheme for mobile phone users

5. A sort of reverse auction website for people buying music online

6. An advertising-based web channel for people to make 3-minute sales pitches for new ideas

7. Short stories sold in cigarette packets

8. A social commerce network to enable people to set up a web shop in minutes.

9. Drill cards for amateur sports coaches

10. A service allowing users to caption online videos

I doubt that the Red Stripe team are eating their hearts out about any of these (though you're probably using one or two of them by now). The message for trend-spotters, unsurprisingly, is that anything with 'sharing' in its description is likely to do well at the moment.

Let's compare those ten ideas with the ideas that Red Stripe received, which they divided up into the following areas:

- An open-authoring, wiki site based around *Economist*-style content and subjects and written by *Economist* readers and experts

- Providing a version of *The Economist* or an educational service for children

- An online prediction/decision/prognosis market

- Finding new ways for *The Economist* to aggregate and present trusted information online (including option to tag and rate articles, overlay data on a world map, etc.)

- An online *Economist* video show

- Making *Economist* data more or less free or available for others to present it differently, show links and patterns, represent it graphically, etc.

- Closely related to the previous idea, suggestions for mash-ups and tagging of *Economist* and related data

- A social networking site for Economist readers

- Putting The *Economist*'s Style Guide online (in its entirety, as there is already a large amount of useful information on the web site).

(Of course there were others. Of these, the best seemed to me to be a Universal Jeans Identification System: give each style of jeans from each manufacturer/company a unique ID, and then compile some sort of searchable database. Different ID numbers could be given for boot cut/straight cut, colour of jeans, men's/women's, etc. That way you could always and easily replace a beloved pair when they fell apart.)

The Red Stripe team described each of these nine idea groups in their blog and then went blogquiet for the next two weeks, while they analysed them. When they posted their next blog, it said:

> We're pretty close to making a decision about what service
> to bring to market. It took many long, sometimes heated

> *debates, and in the end, Javier, our team coach had to play tiebreaker.*
>
> *The bad news is that we have also decided, for the moment, not to make the choice public.*

They had plumped for a social network of sorts, in spite of having recently said, publicly:

> *So a social network for Economist subscribers is indeed quite obvious. Perhaps even so obvious that it would not be very innovative for Project Red Stripe to create one – since* The Economist *is likely to soon start integrating all kinds of community features in its website anyway.*

As Mike said to me towards the end, 'We came full circle. Because we had talked about social networks. The problem is… how do you take the first step?'

Dilemmas:

- How do you take the first step?

Notes – Bright Ideas

- If you're that way inclined, there are, of course, links to all of the sites spotted by springwise in the online version of this book. It also has links to the Project Red Stripe blogs that discuss each of the submitted ideas that is listed here.

Coach Class

Stewart: *'I would have <u>more</u> coaching. Javier's really affected me.'*

I met Javier Bajer at the Royal Society for Arts, by Charing Cross station. In fact it's the Royal Society for the Encouragement of Arts, Manufactures & Commerce. I expect everybody knows that. I didn't. In future, I shall think of it as The Royal Society for Encouragement. There should be more such institutions. In which case, Javier should certainly be in charge of encouragement.

An absurdly busy man, Javier had found two hours to talk to me about his experience as the Project Red Stripe team coach and was telling me that 'it's unavoidable that people will label each other' and that he, for example, couldn't help but see me in a certain light knowing that I was British, middle-aged, rustic, a writer and a wearer of spectacles. 'If,' however, 'you were Uruguayan...' he was continuing when I interrupted him to say that my mother was born and bred in Uruguay. Good coaches, I thought, have good intuition and use it well.

Javier is a man with an avowed mission to change the world by changing the way the people at the top work together and behave towards each other and trusting that the effects of this change will spread virally (what used to be called 'trickle down', but that's a pretty uninspiring metaphor in a ramming speed age). If you're used to coaching some of the top people at some of the world's leading corporations, the idea of changing the world is all in a day's work, so he was perhaps less daunted by the size of Red Stripe's task than the team members themselves – but who wants a timid coach?

The personal lessons with which I came away from our meeting included these:

- that this book, as well as being a piece of fly-on-the-wall reportage about one innovation team could also help to inspire and guide thousands of such teams in the years ahead. (Inspiring)

- that there is a valuable distinction to be drawn between attachment and commitment, which he uses often in his work as a coach. *Commitment* to my new-found goal of helping to guide innovation teams could help me write a balanced, powerful, instructional, energetic, inspiring book. *Attachment* to that goal could lead to me writing it with one eye always on how it would be received, the effect of people's reaction to it on my status, credibility and earning power, etc. (Humbling)

The twin achievement of inspiring and humbling is a remarkable one, and one that he set out to perform with the Red Stripe team (he didn't name that as his intention: it's my subsequent interpretation).

The attachment/commitment distinction was one that Javier stressed when I asked him about Mike's 'not a white paper' recommendation that people should not become personally attached to their preferred ideas. How, I asked, did Javier reconcile this with his (usually successful) attempts to re-energise the team by getting them to identify a project idea that they could be excited and enthused by or a problem that they felt angry about? Didn't the latter, inevitably, require people getting attached to the idea? 'No', he said, 'committed but not attached.' Of course, there's a lot more to it than that, but, as a basis for thinking about ideas, creativity and innovation, it seems like a really useful place for any team to start. It's also another example of the flow of spiritually-grounded ethics into the pragmatic world of business. After all, this approach was presaged by the Buddha, the first of whose Four Noble Truths asserts that not to get what one wants is suffering and that to get what one does not want is suffering and that suffering is brought about by clinging (or attachment).

'Does a team need a coach?' is not a question I asked Javier. But it's one that any putative team member might ask. All the Red Stripe team members I spoke to about it said, categorically, yes. For some of them it seemed that all skilled external intervention was useful. Talking about a day spent with Sally Bibb and David Laird (two Economist Group colleagues), Stewart said, 'having someone external pushing you to do something with your day was fantastic.

It stopped us pussyfooting around.' I did, however, ask Javier about the 'deep communication' that he encouraged in the team in an attempt to build trust and openness. 'Yes', he said, he did intervene when he detected unspoken hostility, resentment and grievances between team members. First, he used tools like a Relationship Map to get people to plot the good and bad relationships within the team, and got them to discuss the results with the aim of airing otherwise unspoken discord. But that was often not enough to overcome tact, discretion or the 'Anglo-Saxon habit' of avoiding confrontation at all cost. When shove came to putsch, he would intervene to say, for example, 'X, how do you feel about the fact that Y has just spent a lot of the meeting challenging your ideas but hasn't put up any of his own?' This kind of intervention requires a) good observation, b) good timing and c) considerable diplomatic skills if it's not to backfire. But it's considerably easier for an external coach or facilitator to do than for one of the team members.

More reasons for having a coach? In Javier's opinion, you're bound to get tensions building up to an unbearable level if you put six people together in a small room (he called it a cockpit with good reason) for six months. 'Human beings', he says, 'need to flock, go out and hunt, then flock again.' Too much flocking and too little hunting causes trouble. I'll say more about the hunting in a minute, but, to deal with the trouble, Javier used 'controlled explosions'. He didn't actually say that he engineered them, but that's pretty much what happened. And affective bomb disposal is not a task to be undertaken lightly with your own colleagues if you don't want to get lynched. Once again, an outside figure will almost always be better equipped to do it.

Whilst we're on the subject, Javier diagnosed too much flocking (I know about the wallpaper thing, but it can't be helped) as one of the reasons for the 'justifiable and understandable' flatness, stuckness or low energy that I was sometimes aware of in the room. (At one point, according to Mike, Javier had said to the team, 'You're just getting by'.) 'It doesn't often happen on Big Brother,' he said, 'because they've got much more physical space.' And it doesn't happen in a typical project team because they only come together periodically for meetings. It's very rare for people to be thrown together in such a small space for such a long time. His remedy in the latter stages was that team members get out into the world to talk about the **Bavaria/Lughenjo** idea, which would get them positive feedback, further ideas and a change of perspective – all helpful in unflattening flatness and unsticking stuckness. It would also require them to explain their idea to others, helping them to focus on the idea's merits and, in the process, 'sell it to themselves' as well as to their audience. The other reason for their stuckness, besides too much flocking, which left them with a lack of connection with other people, was lack of connection with a cause. Hence Javier's efforts to get the team behind a problem they could get angry about or an idea they could get excited by.

All of this provoked me to ask about the ideas-crowdsourcing process (an opportunity for hunting). What did Javier think about it? 'Of course, I wouldn't have allowed it' and the first two months 'was time wasted'. Well that's clear enough. His view is that the team were distracted by the mental model they had, which was that 'the idea exists somewhere and we need to capture it'. So did he think they could have come up with the idea themselves, without asking others? 'No, you need to come out of the current system', which is constrained by existing organisational practice, beliefs and systems. 'You need to be out there in the street, not on the Internet. You need to talk to children... You might get a bit of input from the Web.' So, there's another approach. Personally, I think it downplays the www as a resource, but that reflects my own experience and practice and habits. Anyway, remember equifinality (see page 79).

Finally, I haven't talked about Javier's Leadership Alignment Tool (LAT), which is a set of wooden blocks (and a lot of Cognitive and Behavioural Psychology) that help you consider how well aligned your beliefs/values, intentions, promises and actions/behaviours are. (Do you, for example, believe that angry critical behaviour is inappropriate in the workplace but intend, nevertheless to come down hard on anyone who disagrees with you? Or do you intend and promise to communicate fully and openly, but find yourself not doing so because of lack of time?) It's a rather neat instrument for working out why a team doesn't end up working the way it should, or wants to. Javier described it as 'stabiliser wheels' for a new team.

Ludwig and Tom used precisely this approach to come up with their 'Fresh Air Straw Man'. Unfortunately the Leadership Alignment Tool doesn't include a decision making tool.

If most of this sounds like a plug for team coaches in general, and for Javier in particular, then that's a reflection of the team's reaction to the coaching they received. (Steven: ' The best thing for the team has been Javier.') Though, for balance, I should note that the team's enthusiasm wasn't undiluted. In the process of voting for one Idea when the team was stuck over how to proceed with two (universal primary education and financial literacy for children), Javier gave the five people who were present two votes each. These they could cast as they wished (both for one idea or one for each idea). Three people gave both votes to education. The other two spread their votes. The result: 8:2 for education and everyone had given it at least one vote. A conclusive result. It moved the team on, but glossed over the problem that at least one team member (Ludwig) felt very strongly that financial literacy was the best idea. A trick? Maybe.

And, at another time, some team members felt that Javier's insistence that they should get behind a 'big idea', try and fix a problem that 'made them angry', see this as the one big chance in their lives to make a real difference, was motivated more by Javier's own wish to 'get a big result' than by what was best for the team. Maybe it was both.

Dilemmas:

- Given that most of us are not budding bodhisattvas, how do you get people, in practice, to develop commitment without becoming attached?

- Many tasks in a team really are better done by an external facilitator. But who can possibly justify the expense of having a good one present all or much of the time?

- If human beings do need to flock and hunt alternately, how do you achieve that in a business world that likes to see paid employees at a desk for much of the time? (And if the answer is to hunt via the Internet, how do you give a team experience of children on the street, in that case?)

- And a GCSE debating dilemma: are tricks justified when you need consensus and a decision? Does the end justify the means?

Notes – Coach Class

- On tact and unconstrained communication, see also **Creative Compartments** (page 151).
- I do mean 'affective' in the emotional intelligence sense; not 'effective'.
- There's much more on flocking (unsurprisingly) in **Flocking** on page 191, and on crowdsourcing in **Creativity and Innovation** on page 39.
- See Javier's website (**Webography**) for more about the Leadership Alignment Tool.
- The Fresh Air Straw Man is discussed in **Thunderbirds are Go** on page 145.

Bavaria

After the cantankerous meeting in early April at Mike's house, Javier got the team to vote on the two ideas (helping to achieve universal primary education and improving financial literacy among young people) and they settled on the former. They code-named the idea **Bavaria**. Joanna wasn't there for the vote and was told about the decision the following Monday.

At the time, some team members felt that they'd backed a Lowest Common Denominator idea and Ludwig broadly felt that the idea was 'good enough' but not the best. Though he'd resisted it at Mike's house, he'd seen the team's support for the universal primary education idea and decided that 'resistance was worthless'. He still felt that 'Kids' (the financial literacy plan) was something *The Economist* could do better.

The evolving intention became that of setting up either a charity or a Not-For-Profit organisation to help the UN achieve its millennium goal. This would have a website to facilitate 'frictionless giving'.

At my next visit, the team was well-advanced in its discussions about the cost of the website, whether to let people make donations without first registering, whether to accept advertising, logging donations so you could rank donors as Silver, Gold and Platinum, and so on. There was a new energy in the room as they, at last, worked on a single idea:

Stewart had cut down the 'Do Not Disturb' sign which had been hanging in front of the webcam for several weeks.

Tom announced, 'We shall have massive golden offices and a donkey's foot.'

On the wall were two mock press releases drafted at Javier's suggestion and dated one year ahead. In one, Steven Chiu, *The Economist*'s 'Head of Good' is reported saying that *The Economist* has received praise from the three Bs, Bono, Bill Clinton and Bill

Gates. He says, 'It's nice to meet these people, but the really important thing is doing good.'

Mike and Tom argued briefly about whether to include the specifics of the proposed viral marketing campaigns for **Bavaria** in the business plan. And there was discussion about how many people would register and become donors. Would they need to look outside the pool of *Economist* readers?

> **Tom:** 'If we only get 2,000 people from among *Economist* readers, I'll think we've fucked this.'

> **Stewart:** 'I'm much more pessimistic. I don't think there are loads of *Economist* readers who are thinking, "if only *The Economist* did charity I'd give money to it"'.

Working with a clear goal, the team was suddenly able to overcome obstacles that would previously have led to wrangling and indecision. There was, for example, an ongoing question about whether **Bavaria** should be a charity or not. I listened to Stewart read out long extracts from a Charity Commission report, which seemed to suggest that they couldn't become a charity. No-one else seemed unduly worried. Most of them weren't even listening. I asked how he felt about their reaction:

'They're just carrying on at full speed. I suppose you have to, don't you?'

Continuing to read the Charity Commission report, Stewart cheered himself up with the thought that, 'If they're going to allow the Essex Beekeepers' Association to be a charity, they should allow us.'

This provoked Tom, who has thoroughly realistic aspirations to be a stand-up comedian, to try and think of an Essex Bee joke. He struggled.

Joanna was concerned that they might have bitten off more than they could chew but was 'going with it' enthusiastically. She ventured the thought that, at some level, they might not have finally committed to **Bavaria** being the project, but thought she'd be thrown out of a third floor window if she said so.

Part of the full speed ahead approach was the team's impending presentation of their idea to Gerard Fairtlough, who had come in to advise them at the outset. The presentation was to be a rehearsal for the later presentation to The Economist Group Management Committee. It was intended to highlight areas where they had not done enough research or where their case seemed unpersuasive or unclear. At this stage they were planning to make their presentation to the GMC at its next meeting in mid-June.

Dilemmas:

- Joanna and Ludwig's support for what they felt was, at least, a 'second-best' idea is a good illustration of the 'dissent for the sake of task' problem outlined in **Creative Compartments** on page 151. It was time for the team to unite and get on with implementation – but was this the right idea to unite behind? How do you know when to say 'enough' and stop the discussion and dissent?

Notes – Bavaria

- The cantankerous meeting is described in **Anger** on page 124.
- I can't find an organisation that has employed a 'Head of Good' yet, but there almost certainly is one. (Anthropologists have a term for this, coined by Mary Douglas in *Natural Symbols* [Douglas, 1973, p.xxxv]. It's 'bongo-bongoism' and describes the practice of countering any generalisation – 'eating your grandchildren alive is a universal taboo', for example – with an exception located at some time in the past in a little known tribe.) In any case, it's also perhaps an oblique reference to the Google motto: Don't be evil.

Corporate plants

Joanna: **'Stew…'**

Stewart (whose grip on other languages was tentative and whose favourite foreign phrase was the mysterious **'schappa la dente'**): **'Comment allez-vous?'**

Joanna: **'J'ai un question.'**

Stewart: **'Steady.'**

I notice how some team members use headphones to insulate themselves from the noise of group interactions (and, thereby, exclude themselves from those exchanges). The laptop screen captures the attention; absorbs it. The headphones wrap music – or silence – densely around. Another blanket. The stress ball occupies the hands and much of the available tactile sensation. The occasional barminess of an unsilenced mobile ringtone intrudes. Nobody tuts.

On the central desktop (the real one, not the virtual one) no telephones sing. A grey, three-footed BT device balances on top of two oranges in a silver-coloured wire bowl. Its large central pad reveals it to be a loudspeaker-enabled conference phone and not part of a dubious gift exchange between the crew of the Starship Enterprise and the governing council of Planet Nebulon.

There are, of course, no tissues on the central desktop. There is a row of small green corporate plants in a stained old plant tray behind the door on a safe. The plastic box of Lego survives from the early team-building session. There are two small fire extinguishers and a copy of what the UK Health and Safety Executive deems you should know about current workplace legislation.

Dilemmas:

- A problem familiar to anyone who's ever worked in an open plan office: putting several people round a big desk promotes communication and interaction. But work often requires focus and absorption. Communication becomes disruption. We walk on eggshells or wrap ourselves up, like a hooter in a muffler. How do you foster open communication <u>and</u> creative concentration?

Notes – Corporate Plants

- Tom was occasionally accused of taking home the fruit from this wire bowl and using it to make puddings for girls.

Interviews with horses

Kathy Sierra (who crossed swords for a while with Chris Locke, the co-author of the magnificent *Cluetrain Manifesto*, of which more later) talks a great deal about innovation. Here's a piece from a blog of hers:

> *'Professionals' in any field come in two flavors: Knowledge Sharers and Knowledge Hoarders. The hoarders believe in the value of their 'Intellectual Property'(IP). The products of their mind must be carefully guarded lest anyone steal their precious ideas. But let's face it – if our only 'strategic advantage' is our ideas, we're probably screwed. Or as CDBaby's Derek Sivers put it...:*

> 'It's so funny when I hear people being so protective of ideas. (People who want me to sign an NDA to tell me the simplest idea.) To me, ideas are worth nothing unless executed. They are just a multiplier. Execution is worth millions.'

> *Yes, there are some crucial exceptions, but for most of us, **It's our implementation, not our idea that matters.** Even those who create something revolutionary are still synthesising... still drawing on the work of others, and making a creative leap. But even a big-ass gravel-hauling leap is still a leap, not a physics-violating idea that shimmered into the universe from nothin' but air.*
> *It's how we apply those ideas.*
> *How creative we are.*
> *How useful we are.*
> *How brave we are.*
> *How technically skilled we are.*
> *How we anticipate what our users will love.*
> *How we learn from the ideas and work of others.*

> *And from our (my co-authors and myself) perspective, **it's not about our ideas, it's about what the ideas can do for our users.***

> *Even if we are the only ones to have a specific new and protectable 'idea' (unlikely), the moment we reveal it, everyone else will have it too. The barrier to entry today is way too low to use 'intellectual*

property' as a main advantage. And all too often, we think we have a unique idea only to find that others are – independently – doing the same things.

In spite of the very public fight she had with Chris Locke, Kathy talks much the same language as him. They speak of changing the way corporations do business, of interconnectivity, of the way that the Internet can unlock creative thinking and liberate people to think wildly. And a great deal more.

Chris started the ball rolling by interviewing a horse at length and ended his very first post on what might have been just about the Internet's first blog, with the immortal opt-out box:

> ☐ From time to time we offer to share our list of subscribers with door-to-door aromatherapy salespersons and ritual ax-murderers. If you would prefer that your data not be used in this way, please check the box.

Back to the point. Knowledge Sharers and Knowledge Hoarders.

Project Red Stripe walked this tightrope nervously. They started very openly, blogging everything. The PRS website described what they were doing, how they were recruiting team members, where their offices were. (Indeed, Joanna observed early on that the blog was too close to an introspective diary rather than being one that highlighted issues and ideas.) Their webcam was always on. Then they got the ideas in. They got a little cagey. Acknowledged lots of the ideas. Got involved in some rather public wrangling about whether a six-month subscription to *The Economist* was a suitable reward for someone who gave them a multi-million-moolah (please can someone invent a universal term for currency for occasions like this when it doesn't matter what currency you're talking about, except the Zimbabwean dollar) business idea. Received a shot across the bows from people who are paid to worry about customer perceptions at Economist Tower. Realised that they couldn't be too public if they were going to develop their idea far enough to be able to surprise and delight the GMC. Were told that they shouldn't have gone quiet. Went public again about **Lughenjo**, but cautiously so as not to upset the NGOs they were talking to. Went quiet for the switch to **HiSpace**. Then announced the switch just as they were closing Project Red Stripe.

The way I've described it sounds harsh. But look at it from the other end of the telescope: *The Economist* is a big brand. The magazine doesn't interview imaginary horses and has opt-out boxes that don't mention axe murderers. Red Stripe had to pay attention to these things. Getting closed down or massively alienating their Chief Executive or their readers wouldn't have helped them get a result. They could have spent more time on internal PR to make their case, but that wasn't their job. Perhaps Project Red Stripe needed its own PR department. Perhaps they should have hired someone. But they'd still have had to agree an approach, brief the PR daily, have more meetings. Cul de sac? Another reason for stopping the blog was that it simply took too much time. I watched Ludwig, turned sideways from the desk, writing his blog of 13th March for the entire afternoon. It was, in essence, a defence of the terms and conditions attached to their request for ideas and a response to some of the criticism they'd received from Slashdot. It needed writing. But it didn't need writing.

(On the subject of PR, and if you're not in the business, check out the emerging idea of Open PR, which, in the stress it places on the trustworthiness of employees and the need for honesty in business, could be the brainchild of Christopher Locke and Cluetrain but is actually an emergent property of Web 2.0 and Wikinomics.)

At the other end of the telescope, Red Stripe was adapting and adapting fast. The team were open when they could be, closed when they had to be. At times they were just reacting (although that's been a bad word in business for a long time, it's what we all need to do to stay alive). What Linnaeus called Meteorici adjust their opening and closing times to suit the weather conditions. It seems as good a model as any for an innovation team.

Dilemmas:

- Be completely open on principle? Be secretive sometimes? Be secretive on principle? Wait till an idea is 'well-enough' formed that it won't get shot down? Invite discussion and analysis from the outset?

- If you're going to be very public, delegate the PR job to one of the team? Share it out? Hire someone?

==

Notes – Interviews with Horses

- *The Cluetrain Manifesto* is [Levine, et al., 1999]. It's still a riveting and inspiring book for anyone who thinks about the Internet and for marketing people in particular.
- The excerpt is from Kathy Sierra's blog of 10th June, 2006. See *Passionate* in the **Biography**.
- The point about knowledge sharers and knowledge hoarders ties in closely with what Dwayne Melancon calls the Plentiful Attitude and the Scarcity Attitude (see **Dogging**, page 43).
- Chris Locke and Cathy Sierra crossed swords about violent and misogynistic comments made towards her in blogs co-founded (but not written) by him. She cancelled a public talk because she felt her life was at risk. The language used was on a par with that you'll hear at the crease on any day of a test match involving the Australian cricket team. Which etiquette should prevail on the Internet – dinner party or cricket match?
- An NDA is a non-disclosure agreement.
- See the online version of this book for the Open PR link.
- As the home page at **www.wikinomics.com** explains:

   In the last few years, traditional collaboration – in a meeting room, a conference call, even a convention center – has been superceded by collaborations on an astronomical scale.

   Today, encyclopedias, jetliners, operating systems, mutual funds, and many other items are being created by teams numbering in the thousands or even millions. While some leaders fear the heaving growth of these massive online communities, Wikinomics explains how to prosper in a world where new communications technologies are democratising the creation of value. Anyone who wants to understand the major forces revolutionising business today should consider Wikinomics their survival kit.

State of Vigilance: Heightened

Stewart: *'There are often two or three of us doing something and the rest of us are hanging around. I don't mind hanging around.'*

The National School of Government (formerly the UK's Civil Service College) had a sign on each building saying, 'State of Vigilance: Heightened'. The word 'heightened' was on a dial, so you could select the appropriate state – a bit like a [NO] VACANCIES sign at a Bed and Breakfast. I was unsure what to do in the face of this information. Should I tense slightly, to match the vigilance in the environment? Or could I relax, knowing that all that stuff was taken care of?

The Newmarket Room in Northcote House at the National School of Government is a pale sick green with a de Vere logo-infested carpet and complimentary wi-fi access. There's a cheap clock on the wall and a framed print of the start of a horse race and a buzz. Back in February, Tom had said, 'I'm really excited about when we get to the really hard work stage.' It felt like the hour had come.

The team (sans Mike) is making hurried, last-minute changes to the 'Business Plan Lite'. Ludwig wrote it over Saturday night in Berlin ('when else can you work with kids around?'). There's some debate about which of the ice-cream consumption statistics to use – the US figure or the global figure (they're planning to compare the cost of achieving universal primary education to the money we spend on ice cream each year).

Stewart is fixing errors in one of the spreadsheets. Joanna is printing a revised version of the Business Plan. Steven is working on the final version.

Everyone's looking smart. Shirts: Stew's has little checks, Tom's has stripes, Steven's has big checks, Ludwig's is white and short-sleeved. Joanna has a grey top with outsize buttons. Not a pair of jeans in sight.

At the start of lunch, Gerard is given the Business Plan to read in preparation for the afternoon presentation. He reads it.

Back in The Newmarket Room after lunch, Mike has two glasses of water balanced on the television as he prepares to make the presentation. Tom organises the space. Steven briefs Mike on final changes to the wording. Gerard arrives and Joanna gets him a cup of tea. Stewart gives the slides a final check. Between them, the team have created a sense of urgency.

Mike makes the presentation. Shakily to start with, but well.

Gerard responds and Ludwig, Joanna and Tom all make notes. Joanna looks slightly puzzled. She comes with a puzzled look as standard. As if she didn't quite catch the beginning of the last sentence. Ludwig can look weary. He sits turned sideways, as usual, and smiles from time to time as he listens to Gerard's comments, which seem to be unconditionally positive. Gerard leans well back in his chair. Tom sits low in his. Joanna sits up.

> The explorer and the pioneer stand up; the prisoner and the slave crouch; the saint leans forward, the overseer and magnate lean back. The marshal rides, Hamlet walks, Shylock extends the hands, Carmen requires the weight on one foot, hands on hips, eyes over the shoulder... Guilt, craft, vision, meanness, ecstasy and lure appear in certain arrangements of arms, hands, shoulders, neck, head and legs. Thus the stuff of the ages goes into man's thinking, is interpreted, and comes out in movement and posture again.

Gerard raises some questions and notes of caution: 'The site could run away with itself and lose touch with the broader picture.' 'Attempts to get people on your side are sometimes counter-productive.'

Asked about when they should make their presentation to the GMC, he says, 'I'd present before it's in the public domain... I'd do it as soon as possible.'

Afterwards, Steven felt that Gerard wasn't very challenging, while Mike said that he was, but in a gentle way. An interesting example of different perceptions of the same event, reflecting perhaps cultural or individual differences, or both.

Mike noticed that 'the rigour of working to a deadline is really helpful. We need to do it more often.'

(Much later, Gerard said to me, 'I think they expected me to be nastier to them than I was,' which was almost certainly true. They were probably looking for a foretaste of the kind of probing critique that they would receive from the Group Management Committee. This reminded me very forcibly that much of the world still does business in a thoroughly aggressive and antagonistic way. Sally Bibb has much to say on the subject, observing that, 'It's hard to understand how heads of industry can act so pugnaciously in a world where we know and understand very well what it takes to be a good leader and what is necessary to take people with you. There is so much research and the findings are clear.' The result of the pugnacious approach, she continues, is that you 'end up with employees who are afraid of making mistakes, taking risks and telling the truth – all for fear of retribution'. This is life as it is still lived in a Theory X world, an approach that is fundamentally at odds with creativity and innovation.

It is also profoundly at odds with the millennials (otherwise known as Generation Y) who will be driving that innovation from now on. As a leading consultancy in this field says of the issues raised in recruiting, developing and retaining members of the wired generation, 'Attitudes to authority, work/life balance, corporate responsibility as well as the ways and methods of communicating are just some of the areas which are affecting the future of work.'

That sounds like stating the obvious, but underneath it lies a concern with the implications of the extraordinary changes that have taken place in the last 20 years. As a generation reared on email and mobile phones, computer games, personal webspace, MSN and Craigslist enters the employment market, it does seem unlikely that they'll work doggedly for the organisational status quo.

Back in the presentation room, Ludwig noted, 'There was one show-stopper in there. We need to deal with it straight away. It was, if the charities don't want to work with us.'

Outside Northcote House, are two enormous cast iron door knockers. They're mounted on the two columns on either side of the door rather than on the door itself, so they knock into masonry, not onto a metal plate. Each of these massive knockers each carries a representation of a woman sucking on or blowing into a tube which leads into the vast, ornate lamp set in front of the knocker. Tom and Stewart, who are hanging around outside while the others sort out their accommodation, wonder whether she is inhaling the gas from the light.

Knockers too high to reach, too heavy to lift, unable to make a sound, having gas sucked out of them. Can you see how this chapter is going to end?

No, nor can I.

Dilemmas:

- If you tell others that you're being vigilant, does it make them more or less vigilant themselves? What implications does this have for an innovation team?

Notes – State of Vigilance: Heightened

- The quote about the explorer and the pioneer is from *Beyond Words* [Moore & Yamamoto, 1988].
- Sally's critique of pugnacious leaders is from her *Guardian* article [Bibb, 2006].
- Theory X (as explained by the man who first proposed it as one of two principal views of people at work – [McGregor, 1960]) assumes that the average person dislikes work and tries to avoid it as far as possible, doesn't want responsibility, would rather follow than lead, is self-centred and resists change. Essentially, Theory X assumes that people work only for money and security.

- The Generation Y consultants are TalentSmoothie, to be found at www.talentsmoothie.com.

- There's a nice explanation of the attitude of millennials to work in Per Bäckius's essay (Bäckius, 2002). He quotes a Swedish entrepreneur saying, '... we are now dealing with a new individual – a new consumer and a new employee. The new individuals do not take orders and distrust authority. They are in charge of their own lives and make their own choices. They take crap from no one. You have to design your business as well as your organisation in accordance with their dispositions otherwise they will leave you.'

Flocking

Stewart: **'I'm going to work from home tomorrow, unless anyone has any objections.'**

Joanna: **'We'll miss you.'**

On the way home from hearing Javier talking about people's need to flock from time to time, which he related to the tensions that can build in the course of one family Christmas dinner, never mind over six months in a cockpit, I was reading Arie de Geus's *The Living Company*. In it he quotes Allan Wilson's suggestion that accelerated evolution takes place intragenerationally in certain species when three characteristics are present:

- Innovation – the capacity to invent new behaviour.

- Social propagation – the capacity to transmit skills through direct communication rather than genetically.

- Mobility – the capacity to move around as individuals, to come together into flocks, and to move as a flock.

Arie then makes two key assertions. The first is that, 'no one can "command" a bird to flock in a certain direction, because the travel pattern of the flock emerges from its own movement'. We all know that choreographing directional flocking in geese, cats or fish is hard. But the idea that the next movement emerges from the current one is less obvious. In an innovation team, as in all things, it may be helpful to start from movement rather than from stasis.

The second assertion is that 'human organisations have resources for evolution'. No quibbling with that. But he expands on this by saying, 'surely, corporate life is not a Greek tragedy in which the outcome is hardwired into the characters by the Olympian gods, and the play can climax only in its inevitable tragic ending'.

To take his second assertion first, I'm not so sure. The error, fatal flaw or *hamartia*, which leads Oedipus unwittingly but unerringly to the awful climax of killing his father and marrying his mother, is still used in contemporary psychotherapy when talking about the scripts that people act out in their lives. Sometimes it really does seem that an individual is hell-bent on his own destruction or on making the same mistakes again and again in different relationships. Often we can link this determination to explicit or unacknowledged beliefs that the individual holds about himself. I see no reason not to extend this analysis to organisations, where a group of individuals can hold equally strong beliefs and assumptions about the organisation, its worth, its direction and its likely end. When organisation culture experts talk about culture as 'the way we do things around here', they refer to a whole range of values and beliefs that inform every aspect of an organisation's operation and can define, unless they are openly challenged, how that organisation will end its days.

But to return to Arie's first assertion about directional flocking, I learnt that Craig Reynolds was working two decades ago on replicating flocking behaviour with computer modelling. In thinking about the steering behaviours of a boid (a computer simulation of a single flocking creature) he concluded that three factors are at play:

- Separation: steer to avoid crowding local flockmates.
- Alignment: steer towards the average heading of local flockmates.
- Cohesion: steer to move towards the average position of local flockmates.

It seems to me that separation, alignment and cohesion (which, at first sight, look interestingly contradictory) may be behaviours or inclinations that can be seen at work in many situations from a holiday beach to an artistic movement to a business. They were certainly in operation at Red Stripe, both in terms of the team members' working relationships with one another and in terms of the team's relationships with the outside world.

Furthermore, I found that Bryan Coffman has written about the application of some of these principles to the organisation. Talking about Knowledge Nodes or Knodes, he suggests some rules that each Knode follows in a web or flock of Knodes:

- *If another Knode does something you value, emulate it.*

- *Send regular "here's my current state" messages – communicate your current state to your neighborhood.*

- *Hunt for and discover resources and opportunities. Once discovered, communicate these as a part of your current state message.*

- *Look outward to identify new ideas, toys, tools and techniques. Once identified, communicate these as a part of your current state message.*

- *Tell the story of the purpose of the web to new Knodes you run into (which may or may not be a part of the current web/flock that you belong to).*

- *Family and immediate neighborhood come first.*

- *Critical mass:*

    If the neighborhood flock is too small for critical mass, join another one.

    If the neighborhood flock is too large and noisy, split off.

- *Align with and converge upon the currently highest wealth-generating opportunity (from your value vantage point) that you are aware of, based on current state messages you receive from other Knodes.*

- *Always ship a product from your experiences to your local neighborhood. A product is actually a specific subset of a current state message.*

- *Reply to current state messages you think are valuable, even if it's just to say, 'thanks, that was valuable'. DON'T respond to current state messages which you think are not valuable.*

Now there's an interesting prescription for an innovation team. Again, the rules can apply to the way team members work together and to the way the team as a whole relates to the organisation it works for and to the outside world.

- Emulation reminds us that the incremental approach to change may be more useful than the quantum leap.

- Current state messages sound like Gerard Fairtlough's suggestion that we write things down.

- Hunting for resources and opportunities sounds like a more practical approach than hunting for an idea. It might help to avoid becoming-whale syndrome.

- Looking outward was obvious for this team; less obvious for many others. And looking for toys is like talking to children.

- Telling the story is what Javier urged the team to do when they were getting stuck.

- Family first is, amongst other things, a reminder of the issues that some team members faced whilst working so far from their families.

- Critical mass gives us a guide for the size of the team and the business of working in one room.

- Focusing on wealth-generating opportunities would have changed the team's direction at the time it was thinking about starting a charity.

- Shipping a product from your experiences is a way of describing Mike's not-a-white-paper, which could perhaps be extended to include a reminder of the unexploited ideas that the team considered.

- The formula for replying to current state messages might have been a helpful guide for Red Stripe when they were receiving ideas at the crowdsourcing stage.

Dilemmas:

- The theory of flocking seems to make very good sense and is intrinsically appealing. Web 2.0 is all about flocking and the transmission of memes. As we've noted, the team was doing a great deal of online flocking. But many extremely creative people find flocking anathema. Recruit hermits or flockers to your team? And if you opt for both, how do you get them to work together?

- Like what used to be called surfing the web, telling the story, transmitting and acknowledging current state messages, hunting and emulating all require huge amounts of time. I discuss in **Interviews with Horses** (page 182) whether a team like this perhaps needs one person working full time on PR, but maybe it would also be useful to separate out those responsible for all these necessary flocking behaviours and those responsible for making a plan and creating a new business?

Notes – Flocking

- Allan Wilson's theories are clearly set out in [De Geus, 1999] and in the article linked to from the electronic edition of this book. If you're a British reader of a certain age, his theories also neatly explain how blue tits learnt to drink the cream from your pinta (I appreciate that this sentence will make no sense to many readers).
- There's much more on Craig Reynolds's work at [Reynolds, 2008].
- On Knodes, see [Coffman, 1997].
- I talk about the team's incremental approach in **Profitability and Systems Thinking** (page 89), about becoming-whale in **Becoming Whale** (page 1), about talking to children and telling the story in **Coach Class** on page 171. For other cross-references in this chapter, please see the electronic version.

A Facebook for Good

Tom: *'We started off doing this for hippy reasons, couldn't make it work and now we're going to make money from it. That seems really cool to me. I like it.'*

When I arrived on the 14th May, it was to be greeted by the site of Tom without his moustache and with a black eye acquired whilst playing rugby. The laptop stands had acquired their own meta-stands, which look like inverted filing trays, to raise them even higher and deal with the back problems some of the team were experiencing. I'm 5'11" and every member of the team was significantly taller than me. It was like working in Holland again, which auxologists claim used to be home to the shortest people in Europe (though these claims have been challenged), but now unquestionably is home to the tallest – apart from the inhabitants of the Dinaric Alps.

Mike had presented the well-developed **Bavaria** idea to the publisher of *The Economist*. His suggestion that they narrow the idea down led the team to abandon the idea of handling money or taking donations and to move to a higher level, where they would gather and present information about different education-related projects, NGOs, etc.

My sense of disappointment at this change of tack was reflected in the rather non-committal replies I got from the team members that I talked to. The energy was low again. People were 'working away' on marketing plans and on getting low-cost or free hosting and software for the site. Nevertheless, this level of 'working away' was proving phenomenally productive compared with what had gone before. Ludwig had been talking to 'key players' in the business. Steven had been researching, amongst many, many other things, the Bill and Melinda Gates Foundation, which they were thinking of approaching for funding. The team's Central Desktop database now housed a mountain of documentation about their meetings, research and other developments. Extensive, confidential documents showed, for example, how visitors would use the website and explained in detail the search and inference engine functionality. Action lists, user guides, mission statements, staffing plans, marketing plans, elevator pitches, NGO meeting reports and business plans were updated hourly. Data was being added faster than you could read it. Mike was to spend the next two weeks presenting their refined ideas to individual members of the GMC so that there would be no surprises when it came to the main presentation to the committee as a whole in June.

Mike arrived back from making a presentation to Helen Alexander.

> **Tom:** 'Was she positive?'.

> **Mike:** 'She was not not positive.'

> **Tom:** 'I'd have thought that was the best news we could possibly have had.'

A little later, at 12.30, Joanna fired up the three-pronged device and telephoned Ludwig, who was in Berlin, so he could join a scheduled meeting. Ludwig wasn't there.

In mid-June Mike and Ludwig finally made their long-awaited presentation to the GMC. Their stated intention was to ask, 'What do we need to do to ensure that you don't say no when we make our final presentation to you in July?' The GMC had dutifully responded with a series of difficult questions including, 'Is *The Economist* the best organisation to do this?' and the team pressed on, mindful of these. Time was getting short and Stewart already realised that one of the two websites he was working on (one being essentially a skills exchange and the other a very, very smart world map) wouldn't be ready by the end of July, when the team was scheduled to disband. There was clearly a problem with the timing – they had to have a 'product' ready at exactly the same time as they made their final presentation to the GMC in late July. Even though Red Stripe's initial brief had been to launch its idea, whatever it might be, without reference to the GMC, the team had not felt able to go ahead with such a sensitive idea without the close involvement of the GMC.

Now the team was motoring, they were using Javier less often than before – even though Mike felt that they weren't working as hard or as long hours as they could. There was a lurch when, based on the GMC's feedback, they decided to abandon the not-for-profit route and make it a commercial business, but the team seemed to come into line quickly and talked as if they had all felt uncomfortable with the not-for-profit idea all along. At this stage, of course, there wasn't much room for disagreement. They would hardly get finished as it was – certainly, there was no time for discussion and no room to change course. (As early as February, Stewart had said in exasperation at how long it could take to talk about things, 'We don't have to spend five hours discussing it. We do it now for 30 minutes and everyone gets timed.')

Another recent decision had been to change the name from 'Bavaria' to 'Lughenjo' – a Tuvetan word meaning 'gift', which provoked the immortal blog line, 'Beware geeks bearing gifts'. **Lughenjo** was to be a 'Facebook for good' and '<u>the</u> place where collective intelligence is used to create market-based solutions to development problems'.

One lurking issue was, 'what would happen on 1st August?'. The project would need to continue and Mike was planning to start a small team to run it. Who would be on it?

Notes – A Facebook for Good

- The auxology stuff makes a bit more sense in the online version.

- Tuveta is, apparently, a language and Webster's has a book of English to Tuveta crossword puzzles. But Bloomsbury's definitive *Dictionary of Languages* doesn't even mention it and Google doesn't find any reference to it apart from Webster's and Project Red Stripe. I assume dictionary publishers invent stuff to protect their copyright, just as cartographers invent topographical features (a friend of mine drew the otherwise unreported Pu-Ding Basin onto a map of China, although more for reasons of boredom and revenge than copyright protection).

Of Topsy and William Zanzinger

In **Interviews with Horses** (page 182) I've talked about the idea of the Project Red Stripe team getting their own PR department. That's just one indication of how easy it is for these things to grow like Topsy.

Two examples of how it could get out of hand follow:

1. In March, Joanna posted a blog about reasons why the Project Red Stripe idea-gathering email campaign had to be very carefully planned and thought through. (There's more about it in **On Experts and Expertise**, page 202). The next day, just before lunch, the following comment was received and published on the blog:

   So now you're sending out spam as well as phishing for other people's ideas?

Just after lunch, the following (understandably testy) reply appeared from Mike (not Joanna):

   The emails were sent to a very small sample of Economist Group customers that had specifically asked to receive occasional emails from The Economist Group.

   That doesn't meet most people's definition of spam.

Doing your business in public can be a thankless task.

2. Earlier in the month, Ludwig submitted a long post to the public blog about the response they'd had from Slashdot and others. After spanking his readers with a little dialectical materialism, Ludwig cantered through some of the most common criticisms heaped upon Red Stripe's decision not to publish the ideas submitted by their readers and to reward the originator of the best idea with a six-month subscription to *The Economist*. (Bob Dylan admirers and students of Christopher Ricks will remember the breathless pause in the lines:

> *And handed out strongly, for penalty and repentance,*
> *William Zanzinger with a…… six-month sentence)*

On the way, Ludwig – by agreement with the rest of the team – also publicly spanked Stewart for having submitted anonymously to the debate on Slashdot.

This and other posts of his drew a generally furious response along the lines of 'You, my dear friends, suck'. Which provoked Mike to respond with further justifications.

Here, as elsewhere, the team was sometimes reduced to wondering why they couldn't just get on and do stuff.

Doing your business in public can also be a time-consuming task. Even though anthropologists try not to, the rest of the world will gladly leap to judgement. It's where we're all most comfortable.

Perhaps, in the end, Oliver Burkeman had the answer when he wrote this in the Guardian about a TV film by Adam Curtis called The Trap:

> *The most perceptive comment on the situation comes, in Curtis's film, from a beleaguered bus conductor, in archive footage used as a counterpoint to the visionary talk of targets and markets and freedom. It could serve as a general diagnosis of the problem of how best to approach politics, psychology, culture – the lot. 'Anybody that deals with the public, you can never win,' he says, flatly. 'You can never win when you deal with the public. Never.'*

Certainly, much of the response to Red Stripe's search for ideas is underpinned by assumptions and prejudices about how an organisation like The Economist Group, or innovators like this team, or capitalists in general are likely to operate. Certainly, if you keep on telling people they're selfish and calculating, that's how they'll behave. 'We … come to believe,' as Adam Curtis says in The Trap, 'that we really are the strange, isolated beings that the cold war scientists had invented to make their models work.'

So, another question has to be: how can a commercial organisation like The Economist Group behave fairly in this context? How can we commercialise the lichens in your rainforest, the knowledge of your traditional medicine practitioners, the ideas of your creative artists fairly and ethically?

The answer is that you can't. The commercialised eventually have to get savvy about exploiting their exploiters (if you frame it in that language). We have enough trouble working out how high-earning husbands can ethically draw on the support of low- or no-income wives, and how the latter can leverage their redundancy payments when the relationship reaches full term. And we have enough trouble working out how young porn stars can commercialise their skills and assets without exploiting fat, bald, old, rich men. Or is it the other way round?

In the end, the only thing was for The Economist Group and the world to trust the six people on Project Red Stripe to do the right thing. And that's an act of trust that we have to commit to hundreds of times a day in hundreds of different situations.

Certainly, all the team members were aware of Google's informal corporate motto 'Don't be evil', which is so often rendered as 'Do no evil' (perhaps in an effort to avoid the painful naiveté of the real thing). More than that, the team visibly relaxed at those times when they had settled on a philanthropic mission. Of course, there were still reservations about whether it was the right sort of philanthropy or whether it should be not-for-profit, but 'doing good' was always the most comfortable place for the team to be ideologically.

Notes – Of Topsy and William Zanzinger

- Joanna's blog post is on the Project Red Stripe blog, dated 20th March, 2007. Ludwig's is dated 13th March.
- The *Guardian* article is [Burkeman, 2007].

On Experts and Expertise

The exigency of sending a fax in 2007 (see **Alexander Bain and the Fax Machine**, page 163) raises other questions about the presence of experts with specialised knowledge of the design and maintenance of websites, information and magazine marketing, writing and so on. There was a natural tendency for the experts to be asked, or to volunteer, to undertake tasks within their 'special subject'. At times, this was clearly helpful. Joanna, for example, because she already knew the ins and outs of the different postal and email customer databases held by the different Economist Group businesses, was able to shortcut the considerable amount of research that would otherwise have been needed to find out how best to approach a representative sample of the Group's customers.

On reflection, though, it seems to me that the innocent eye of a non-specialist might have lighted on unexpected possibilities which the expert eye overlooked. Perhaps it wasn't necessary to select a representative sample. Joanna herself spotted this when she alerted the others to the fact that she was going to be less than scientific in her determination of the size of samples from each list.

In fact, she proposed 'gut-rounding' the numbers rather than doing a precise, statistical calculation and checked this with the others present. Only Stewart answered, announcing that he felt there was 'plenty of room for gut-rounding'. It seems to me likely that someone without a marketing training would never have considered the niceties of statistical sampling and the project would have been none the poorer.

And, at other times, things might have moved more quickly if, for example, the business of writing most documents had *not* been handed to the resident journalist. *Economist* correspondents surely feel some obligation to meet the expectation (both their own and that of their colleagues) that they will write exquisitely, even in situations where carefully crafted prose is not required.

This was also Mike's analysis. In late February he told me that he didn't want the 'expert' on the team to do all the writing or all the marketing or all the programming, but it subsequently proved difficult to change this pattern.

Another way of looking at this conundrum of the expert is offered by Carol Dweck. As we saw in **Mindsets** (page 75), the issue is whether you view your capabilities (for example, as a writer or a speaker or a researcher) as a fixed character or personality trait or, rather, as something that you believe you can develop and refine. When faced with obstacles, fixed-mindset individuals tend to be much more concerned with performance and showing that they are 'as good as they're cracked up to be'. By contrast, the learning-driven person will be more likely to see obstacles as opportunities for growth.

As Russell Ackoff has observed,

> *Doing something right can only confirm what one already knows or believes; one cannot learn from it. However, one can learn from making mistakes, by identifying and correcting them. Nevertheless, making a mistake is frowned upon in most organisations, from school on up, and often is punishable. To the extent that recognition of mistakes is suppressed, so is learning.*

So perhaps, in conclusion, one of the most important skills for members of a team like this one is to know when doing something 'well enough' is all that's required. As Donald Winnicott saw in another context, 'the good enough mother' enables the developing child to make a smooth transition to a reasonable sense of independence and self-reliance (precisely because the good enough mother often – but not always – meets the needs of the child). In a project like this, the struggle for perfection eats time and energy and may achieve little.

In the same vein, another important skill is surely to be able to call upon, and communicate effectively with, experts outside the team.

But that, too, is only part of the picture. We've seen that Joanna would question repeatedly and fruitfully whether there was really a demand for whatever product or service the team was currently contemplating and ask the simple question, 'Who's it for?'.

Equally, it's clear that, under pressure, the team benefited from being able to draft, amend and polish a business plan 'in-house' and without the need for time-consuming input from external advisers.

More on precision

I've talked about the team's occasional desire for unnecessary precision (whether in language or statistics). The same could be said of the whole business of setting up a prototype 'idea-gathering' exercise, whereby the team would test and refine its process for requesting, receiving, filtering, reading, categorising and evaluating new ideas from external sources.

The idea of testing the exercise was to ensure that the processes worked and that nothing untoward would happen that might jeopardise The Economist Group's relationship with its readers, customers and the wider world.

For much of February, Ludwig was writing the emails and announcements, Joanna was deciding where to place ads and send emails, Stewart was working on ways of gathering ideas (including rebranding the Project Red Stripe website), Tom was considering how to sift the ideas they would eventually receive and Steven was devising a schedule for the prototype and real idea-gathering exercises.

In fact, at Mike's suggestion, the team eventually decided to collapse the prototype idea-gathering exercise and the 'real thing' into one. That meant they ran just the prototype exercise, because they were running short of time and because they realised that most ideas would fall into a handful of categories – so that receiving a few hundred ideas would be as useful as receiving a few thousand.

Now it's easy to say with hindsight that the weeks spent refining the email and the ads and devising elaborate ways of evaluating each new Idea was were largely wasted.

Perhaps more interesting is that most, if not all, the team members recognised this at the time. In fact, throughout February (the idea-gathering started on the 5th March) some of them were saying not only that their planning was unduly time-consuming and detailed, but that the whole idea-gathering process was unnecessary:

Stewart was frustrated by their self-generated bureaucracy – 'If we set up a Red Stripe community then we'll have to have another discussion first about how to set up the community.' He also said he thought Tom's Regent's Park idea was 'good enough to go with… Let's learn as we go.'

Tom thought they could do it more easily – 'If I went to TechMeme and followed all those links, I could come back with ten cool things The Economist Group could do each day. And I think any of us could do that.'

And again – 'Me and a feed reader would be my ideal way of coming up with an idea.'

Tom was also struck in late February by how much they could do already. He felt they had 'a huge backlog of ideas'. Mike's response was cautious. 'That's "nearly" stuff'. He wanted to get to a 'higher level' to find more original ideas that were 'further off'. (Though, privately, he said that he didn't want to be the one to say that an idea wasn't innovative enough. He wanted the team to agree that between themselves.)

Mike was confident in the team's creative ability: 'If you put the six of us in the right place for a day, we could come up with 200 ideas', and frustrated that it wasn't being used: 'We do need to catch up on creativity within the team. We've spent an awful lot of time on gathering ideas from outside.'

Joanna, who types faster than anyone else in the team, posted to the Red Stripe public blog in March as follows:

In the past two weeks, I often have found myself explaining to my Project Red Stripe colleagues that any 'hold ups' or complications with 'sending out an innocent email' to clients is not our old colleagues trying to plot against us and be difficult, but rather 'the way business is done'.

There are good and fair reasons underlying most things, but the legalities and technicalities invariably frustrate impatient trail blazers, like ourselves. We can't change everything to suit our needs. Rather, we need to learn how to make the system work for us.

Even from this distance, that sounds like a response to frustration and impatience from the rest of the team.

As early as the 7th February Steven said he was 'tempted to do it dirty and just post the Call for Ideas' (which wouldn't actually be made public until a month later).

'But I won't.'

'Why not?', I asked him.

'Because it would hurt the team.'

Ludwig was clear that they needed to wait and shouldn't just launch into idea-gathering. 'We could screw ourselves.'

But, in spite of this general consensus, the idea-gathering process had developed a momentum of its own and the juggernaut rolled on. It seemed that there wasn't room for their combined intuition to be heard and acted on. To that extent, the term 'gut-rounding' is particularly apposite. It reflects the idea of working on 'gut feel', which the team as a whole seemed to find too unscientific, even when their guts were sending out clear signals.

In February, I wrote in the Triarchy Press blog about gut-rounding:

Maybe the eventual book on Project Red Stripe should be about how scientific to be. Or the need to start off scientific in order to break the rules later. I'm thinking of an article for

*Harvard Business Review, followed by a lucrative, franchise
for management consultants. Anyway, I've registered
gutrounding.com.*

Dilemmas:

- Expert knowledge can save you an enormous amount of research and preparation time. But, in feeling that they've got something to prove, the expert owners of that expert knowledge can waste you a lot of time.

- Intuition isn't very scientific, but it can also save you a lot of time. Arguably, most success in business depends on it.

- Good enough is often better than perfect. But not always.

Notes – On Experts and Expertise

- Professor Ackoff's observations on mistakes are taken from *Management f-Laws* [Ackoff, 2006(a)].
- TechMeme and Triarchy Press are in the **Biography**.

Those ideas in full

Regent's Park, 5th February 2007

Steve's presentation was not so much a thought-out idea as a gathering of thoughts. Many *Economist* readers, he supposed, would have sent a letter to the editor and would have moved from being communication Luddites to being heavy Internet users, but probably wouldn't download a podcast.

Were there any low-hanging fruits, perhaps an 'online weekend companion', perhaps a sort of digital *Intelligent Life* (*The Economist*'s 'engaging lifestyle magazine')? Perhaps there were synergies to be derived from combining data from *The Economist*'s 'World In' and 'Cities' Guide', with local community information and blogs? Perhaps a way could also be found to secure weekend advertising through a new service like this?

Subsequent discussion focused on covering leisure, presenting advertising in a more relaxed environment and easing the transition into the digital life.

Tom used chairs to display his hand-written posters (PowerPoint happily wasn't possible in the park). Influenced in particular by Netvibes' web content aggregator and personalised portal service and the way in which he consumed the web, he presumed that this kind of behaviour would become more widespread.

He proposed an 'Economist Reader' homepage service, which would combine comments by magazine readers on *Economist* articles, a bookmark feature (like de.licio.us) to enable users to find out what other *Economist* readers are looking at on the web, a community-based service echoing digg pages for citizen journalists, an 'Economist Sandbox' in which readers could play with *Economist* data and repackage them and a profile page where users could put up their CV, Facebook-style.

There was much discussion of *The Economist*'s intelligent readership, how much it has to say and how much readers have to offer each other.

Stewart's proposal didn't specifically relate to The Economist Group and was much more broad-brush in its approach. It took as its starting point the idea that the Internet is about communication rather than information. Why not, he asked, let people create interest groups and subscriptions within given geographical areas, helping to find local services, a football team or somebody to have a date with? *Economist* readers want to meet other *Economist* readers, and a service like this could be combined with geolocation technology.

Discussion centred around existing services like Twitter and the more business-orientated Linked In and why they were more popular in Asia than in Europe. (The answer, of course, is that China, Japan, Korea and many other countries have their own hugely successful social networking sites).

Joanna's proposal tended to ask questions rather than offer solutions. Before coming up with ideas of what to do, she felt the team should ask things like:

What do people need?

Should they try to do something for a lot of people or only for a specific group?

What can The Economist Group do to fulfil people's fundamental needs?

Everyone agreed that this was an important corrective to the previous discussion they'd been having.

Ludwig's idea, as you'll have guessed, was 'Economist.kids'. He proposed using *The Economist*'s data, skills, resources, reputation and values to create an *Economist*-like service aimed at a much younger audience. It could include a moderated Wiki, advise on job seeking, writing and all aspects of learning as well as offering financial and political information and news.

Much of the discussion was around how to commercialise this service without alienating the target audience.

It was very early on and Mike, in leader/facilitator role, didn't bring a proposal to the park.

Following these ideas through the project, you'll have noticed that Ludwig's Economist.kids proposal made it through to the last two in April, largely due to its author's enthusiasm for the project. Or, as his Myers-Briggs profile said: 'May appear so unyielding that others are afraid to approach or challenge them.'

When the **Bavaria/Lughenjo** idea emerged, centring on universal primary education and a broader philanthropy exchange, it had no real roots in any of the above ideas (except that *Intelligent Life* has a strong philanthropy theme), although it was the result of returning to Joanna's 'what do people need?' approach. But the final **HiSpace** social/knowledge network proposal had obvious roots in Tom's idea and in some of the discussions they'd had in the park in early February.

Notes – Those Ideas in Full

- Most of the sites and services referenced here are listed in the **Webography** at the end of the book. Of course, it's easier to find them all from the online version at www.projectredstripe.blogspot.com

- The extract from Ludwig's Myers-Briggs profile is quoted by him in his blog and, of course, applies to all INTJs, not just him. (And he didn't ask me to say that, either.)

Bibliography

Ackoff, Russell, Addison, Herbert & Bibb, Sally. *Management f-Laws*. Axminster: Triarchy Press, 2006(a).

Ackoff, Russell. 'Why few organizations adopt systems thinking' at http:// ackoffcenter/blogs.com, 2006(b).

Allan, Dave, et al. *Sticky Wisdom: How to Start a Creative Revolution at Work*. Chichester: Capstone Publishing, 2002.

Allan, Julie, Fairtlough, Gerard & Heinzen, Barbara. *The Power of the Tale*. Chichester: John Wiley, 2002.

Amabile, Teresa. 'How to Kill Creativity' in *Harvard Business Review*, September 1998.

Amabile, Teresa, Hadley, Constance & Kramer, Steven. 'Creativity Under the Gun' in *Harvard Business Review*, August 2002.

Anthony, Scott. 'Diagnosing Red Stripe's Failure' at www.innosight.com/ innovation_resources/insight.html, 2007.

Bäckius, Per. 'Other Work: A Dividual Enterprise' in *Ephemera* 2:4 (2002).

Bateson, Gregory. *Steps to an Ecology of Mind: Collected Essays in Anthropology, Psychiatry, Evolution, and Epistemology*. Chicago: University Of Chicago Press, 1972.

Berne, Eric. *Transactional Analysis in Psychotherapy*. New York: Grove Press, 1961.

Bibb, Sally. *The Stone-Age Company*. London: Cyan Books, 2005.

Bibb, Sally. 'Tough at the Top' in *The Guardian*, 4 March, 2006.

Borges, Jorge Luis. *Labyrinths; Selected Stories & Other Writings*. Donald A. Yates, James E. Irby et al. (tr). New York: New Directions Publishing, 1964.

Burkeman, Oliver. 'Cry Freedom' in *The Guardian*, 3 March, 2007.

Burkeman, Oliver. 'This Column Will Change Your Life' in *The Observer*, 7 July, 2008.

Carr, Nicholas. 'The Ignorance of Crowds' in *Strategy + Business*, May 2007.

Chesbrough, Henry. *Open Innovation*. Boston, MA: Harvard Business School Press, 2003.

Christensen, Clayton. *The Innovator's Dilemma*. New York: HarperCollins, 2000.

Christensen, Clayton. Interview by The Gartner Fellows on www.gartner.com (Accessed January 2008).

Clarkson, Petruska. 'Group Imago and the Stages of Group Development: A Comparative Analysis of the Stages of the Group Process' in *Transactional Analysis Journal* 21:1 (January 1991).

Clarkson, Petruska. *The Achilles Syndrome: Overcoming the Secret Fear of Failure*. Shaftesbury: Element Books, 1994.

Coffman, Brian. 'Rules for "Flocking Behavior"' in the Web' on www.mgtaylor. com. 1997. (Accessed July 2008).

Collins, Jim. *Good to Great*. New York: HarperCollins, 2001.

Culbert, Samuel & Ullmen, John. *Don't Kill the Bosses*. San Francisco: Berrett-Koehler, 2001.

Daft, Richard. *Organization Theory and Design*. St. Paul, MN: West Publishing, 1998.

De Geus, Arie. *The Living Company*. London: Nicholas Brealey Publishing, 1999.

Deleuze, Gilles, and Guattari, Felix. *A Thousand Plateaus: Capitalism and Schizophrenia*. Minneapolis, MN: University of Minnesota Press, 1987.

Deming, W. Edwards. *Out of the Crisis*. Cambridge, MA: MIT Center for Advanced Engineering Study, 1982.

Douglas, Mary. *Natural Symbols*. New York: Vintage Books, 1973.

Douglas, Mary. 'Introduction to Grid/Group Analysis' in *Essays in the Sociology of Perception*. Douglas, M. ed. Boston, MA: Routledge & Kegan Paul, 1982.

Drucker, Peter. *Innovation and Entrepreneurship*. New York: Harper & Row, 1985.

Duboff, Robert. 'The Wisdom of (Expert) Crowds' in *Harvard Business Review*, September 2007.

Dumézil, Georges. *Mitra-Varuna*. Derek Coltman (tr). New York: Zone Books, 1990.

Dweck, Carol. *Mindset*. New York: Random House, 2006.

Economist, 'Early Warning System' in *The Economist*, 24 April, 2008.

Edelman, Gerald. *Second Nature*. New Haven, CT: Yale University Press, 2006.

Egan, Gerard. *Working the Shadow Side*. San Francisco: Jossey-Bass, 1994.

Eno, Brian & Schmidt, Peter. *Oblique Strategies*. London: Shakedown Records/ Brian Eno, 2002.

Fagerberg, Jan, Mowery, David & Nelson, Richard. *The Oxford Handbook of Innovation*. Oxford: Oxford University Press, 2005.

Fairtlough, Gerard. *No Secrets: Innovation Through Openness*. Axminster: Triarchy Press, 2008.

Fairtlough, Gerard. *The Three Ways of Getting Things Done*. Axminster: Triarchy Press, 2007.

Fairtlough, Gerard. *Creative Compartments*. London: Adamantine Press, 1994.

Farber, Michael, Greenspon, Tom and Tucker, Jeffrey. 'The Practical Visionary' in *Strategy & Business*, 10 June 2008.

Fichte, Johann Gottlieb. *Science of Knowledge*. Peter Heath and John Lachs (tr). New York: Appleton-Century-Crofts, 1970.

Gilbert, Daniel. 'If only gay sex caused global warming' in *Los Angeles Times*, 2 July 2006.

Gladwell, Malcolm. *The Tipping Point*. London: Little, Brown, 2000.

Gratton, Lynda, Voigt, Andreas & Erickson, Tamara. 'Bridging Faultlines in Diverse Teams' in MIT *Sloan Management Review*, Summer 2007.

Habermas, Jurgen. *The Theory of Communicative Action*. London: Beacon Press, 1981.

Hamel, Gary & Getz, Gary. 'Funding Growth in an Age of Austerity' in *Harvard Business Review*, July 2004.

Hampden-Turner, Charles & Trompenaars, Fons. *The Seven Cultures of Capitalism*. New York: Currency/Doubleday, 1993.

Hargadon, Andrew. 'The Trouble with Out-of-the-Box Thinking' in *Ubiquity* 4:30 (September, 2003).

Hoban, Russell. *Riddley Walker*. London: Picador, 1982.

Hodge, Stephen et al. *A Mis-Guide to Anywhere*. Exeter: Wrights & Sites, 2006.

Humphrey, Nicholas. *Seeing Red: A Study in Consciousness*. Boston, MA: Harvard University Press, 2006.

Hurston, Zora N. *Their Eyes Were Watching God*. Philadelphia, PA: J. B. Lippincott, 1937.

Ingold, Tim. 'Of string bags and birds' nests' in *The Perception of the Environment* 1:4, (October 2000).

Jacobs, Jane. *Systems of Survival: A Dialogue on the Moral Foundations of Commerce and Politics*. New York: Random House, 1992.

Jenks, C. *Watching Your Step: the History and Practice of the Flaneur in Visual Culture*. London: Routledge, 1995.

Jones, Andrew. *The Innovation Acid Test*. Axminster: Triarchy Press, 2008.

Kanter, Rosabeth Moss. 'Innovation: The Classic Traps' in *Harvard Business Review*, October 2006.

Karp, David & Lincoln, Murray. *Vice President in Charge of Revolution*. New York: McGraw-Hill, 1960.

Kierkegaard, S. *The Concept of Dread*. Walter Lowrie (tr). Princeton, NJ: Princeton University Press, 1957.

Laing, R. D. *Knots*. London: Tavistock Publications, 1970.

Lavelle, Lise. *Amerta Movement of Java 1986-1997*. Lund: Centre for Languages and Literature, 2006.

Leadbeater, Charles. *Living on Thin Air*. London: Viking, 1999.

Levine, Rick, Locke, Christopher, Searls, Doc & Weinberger, David. *The Cluetrain Manifesto*. Cambridge, MA: Perseus Publishing, 1999.

Levitt, Theodore. 'Creativity is not Enough' in *Harvard Business Review* (May-June 1963).

Macrae, Norman. 'Intrapreneurial Now' in *The Economist* (17 April, 1982).

McGregor, Douglas. *The Human Side of Enterprise*. New York: McGraw-Hill, 1960.

Margerison, Charles. *Team Leadership*. London: Thomson, 2002.

Maturana, Humberto & Varela, Francisco. *The Tree of Knowledge: The Biological Roots of Human Understanding*. Boston, MA: Shambhala, 1987.

Melville, Herman. *Moby Dick, or The Whale*. London: Cassell, 1930.

Michael, Donald. *Learning to Plan – and Planning to Learn*. San Francisco, CA: Jossey-Bass, 1973.

Michael, Donald & Anderson, Walter Truett. 'Norms in Conflict and Confusion' in *Journal of Humanistic Psychology*, 29:2, (1989).

Moore, Carol-Lynne & Yamamoto, Kaoru. *Beyond Words*. London: Gordon & Breach Publishers, 1988.

Nakane, Jinichiro and Hall, Robert. 'Ohno's Method' in *Target – The Association for Manufacturing Excellence Magazine*, Vol. 18:1, 2002.

Ogle, Richard. *Smart World*. Boston, MA: Harvard Business School Press, 2007.

Ohno, Taiichi. *Taiichi Ohno's Workplace* Management, Mukilteo, WA: Gemba Press, 2007.

O'Reilly, Tim. 'What is Web 2.0' on www.oreilly.net, (September, 2005).

Panksepp, J. 'The core emotional systems of the mammalian brain' in *About a Body: Working with the Embodied Mind in Psychotherapy*, Wilkinson, H., Payne, H. & Corrigall, J. (eds.), London: Routledge, 2006.

Pateman, Trevor. 'The Erotics of Language' at www.selectedworks.co.uk, 1968 (Accessed, January 2008).

Pavitt, Keith. 'The Process of Innovation' in [Fagerberg et al., 2005].

Peters, Tom. *The Circle of Innovation*. New York: Alfred A. Knopf, 1999.

Powell, Jason & Moody, Harry. 'The Challenge of Modernity' in *Theory & Science*, 4:1, (2003).

Price, Frank. *Right Every Time: Using the Deming Approach*. Aldershot: Gower Press, 1990.

Priesmeyer, H. R. *Organizations and chaos: defining the methods of nonlinear management*. Westport, CT: Quorum Books, 1992.

Rae, Jeneanne. 'The Keys to High-Impact Innovation' in *Business Week*, 27 September 2005.

Raymond, Eric. *The Cathedral and the Bazaar*. Sebastopol, CA: O'Reilly Press, 1999.

Rayner, Alan. *My Achilles Heel: Testimony of a 'Gifted' Child*. http://people.bath. ac.uk/bssadmr/inclusionality/AchillesHeel.html (Accessed January 2008).

Reeve, Sandra. 'The Next Step: Eco-Somatics and Performance', given at The Changing Body (conf.), Exeter University, 2006.

Reeve, Sandra. *The Ecological Body*. Unpublished PhD thesis, University of Exeter, 2008.

Reynolds, Craig. 'Boids'. http://www.red3d.com/cwr/boids/ (Accessed July 2008).

Ricks, Christopher. *Dylan's Visions of Sin*. London: Viking, 2003.

Schneier, Bruce. *Beyond Fear: Thinking Sensibly About Security in an Uncertain World*. New York: Copernicus Books, 2003.

Schumpeter, Joseph. *Capitalism, Socialism and Democracy*. New York: Harper & Row, 1942.

Seery, Michael. Project Red Stripe: A Story of Innovation on www. projectredstripe.com (follow the link from the 19 November, 2007 blog post). (Accessed August 2008).

Seybold, Patty. *Outside Innovation*. New York: HarperCollins, 2006.

Smith, Phil. 'Dread, Route and Time: An Autobiographical Walking of Everything Else'. *Reconstruction* 3:1 (Winter 2003).

Stuter, Lynn. 'The Delphi technique' on www.seanet.org (Accessed January 2008).

Surowiecki, James. *The Wisdom of Crowds*. New York: Random House, 2005.

Taleb, Nassim Nicholas. *The Black Swan: The Impact of the highly improbable*. New York: Random House, 2007.

Tapscott, Don & Williams, Anthony. *Wikinomics*. London: Penguin, 2006.

Tate, William. *The Organisation Shadow-Side Audit*. Axminster: Cambridge Strategy Publications, 2008.

Taylor, Frederick. *The Principles of Scientific Management*. New York: Harper, 1911.

Tett, Gillian. 'Office Culture' in *Financial Times*, London, 20 May 2005.

Thompson, Michael. *Organising and Disorganising*. Axminster: Triarchy Press, 2008.

Tolle, Eckhart. *The Power of Now*. Novato, CA: New World Library, 1999.

Tuckman, Bruce. 'Developmental Sequence in Small Groups' in *Psychological Bulletin*, 63, 1965.

Universal McCann. 'When Did we Start Trusting Strangers?' at http://www.universalmccann.com/Assets/strangers_reportLR_20080924101433.pdf, 2008 (Accessed September 2008).

Vaill, P. B. *Managing as a performing art: new ideas for a world of chaotic change*. San Francisco: Jossey-Bass, 1991.

van der Heijden, Kees. *Scenarios: The. Art of Strategic Conversation*. New York: Wiley, 1996.

van Deurzen, Emmy. *Existential Counselling and Psychotherapy in Practice*. London: Sage Publications, 2002.

Von Bertalanffy, Ludwig. *General System Theory: Foundations, Development, Applications*. New York: George Braziller Inc., 1968.

Vulpian, Alain de. *Towards The Third Modernity*. Axminster: Triarchy Press, 2008.

Winnicott, D. 'Transitional objects and transitional phenomena' in *International Journal of Psychoanalysis*, 34, 1953.

Zeldin, Theodore. *Conversation: How Talk Can Change Our Lives*. London: The Harvill Press, 1998.

Blography

Ackoff Center – http://ackoffcenter.blogs.com – Systems Thinking and Russell Ackoff

BuzzMachine – www.buzzmachine.com – Jeff Jarvis on publishing and the media

Chetan Dhruve – http://dhruve.blogspot.com – Why your boss is programmed to be a dictator

Clear Space Thinking – http://connectiveera.blogspot.com – Different ways of thinking about business

Completetosh – www.completetosh.com – Neil McIntosh on innovation and media

Connective Era – http://connectiveera.blogspot.com – Leadership and organisations

Curious Cat Management Improvement – http://management.curiouscatblog.net – Management improvement

Dwayne Melancon – www.genuinecuriosity.com – New ideas, new technology, new thinking

Fedoral Reserve – http://fedoralreserve.wordpress.com – Tom Shelley's blog

Genuine Curiosity – www.genuinecuriosity.com – Getting things done

How to Save the World – http://blogs.salon.com/0002007/ – Dave Pollard's business and environmental blog

Open… – http://opendotdotdot.blogspot.com – Open source, open content

Open Source – http://freethinkr.wordpress.com – Open business models and innovation

Outside Innovation – http://outsideinnovation.blogs.com – Patty Seybold on innovation

P2P Foundation – http://blog.p2pfoundation.net – Peer to Peer practices

Paid Content – www.paidcontent.org – Media and digital content

Passionate – http://headrush.typepad.com – Kathy Sierra on user communities and innovation

Project Red Stripe – www.projectredstripe.com/blog – The Team's public blog.

Project Red Stripe - www.projectredstripe.blogspot.com – The online version of this book

Rageboy – www.rageboy.com/blogger.html – From the author of *The Cluetrain Manifesto*

Sean Murphy – www.skmurphy.com/blog – Software start-ups

Seth Godin – http://sethgodin.typepad.com/seths_blog – Business and marketing

Slashdot – http://slashdot.org – News for nerds

Slow Leadership – www.slowleadership.org/blog – What's wrong with work

Steve Pavlina – www.stevepavlina.com – personal development for smart people

Stewsnooze – www.stewsnooze.demon.co.uk – Stewart Robinson's blog

Stowe Boyd – www.stoweboyd.com – New media

Strange.Corante – http://strange.corante.com – Suw Charman on blogging, wikis, etc.

Techmeme – www.techmeme.com – Technological innovation

The Practice of Leadership – www.thepracticeofleadership.net – All about leadership

Triarchy Press – http://triarchypress.blogspot.com – On organisations

Wikinomics – www.wikinomics.com/blog – Collaboration

World Editors Forum – www.editorsweblog.org – Newspapers

Webography

Bruce Schneier – www.schneier.com – security and cryptography.

Central Desktop – www.centraldesktop.com – project collaboration tools.

Corporate Anthropology – www.antropologi.info/antromag/ – article collection.

Craig Reynolds – www.red3d.com/cwr/boids/ – boids and flocking.

Delicious – http://del.icio.us/ – social bookmarking web service for storing, sharing, and discovering web bookmarks.

Digg – http://digg.com – a content-sharing, social media website.

Financial Times Executive Forums – www.ftexecutiveforums.com – social networking for big cheeses.

Javier Bajer – www.possibilate.com/ – the leadership alignment tool.

John Seely Brown – www.johnseelybrown.com – you guessed it.

Linked In – www.linkedin.com – business oriented social networking site.

M. G. Taylor – www.mgtaylor.com – 'Group Genius' and the design oriented organisation.

Netvibes – www.netvibes.com – personalised web start page.

Open Innovation – www.openinnovation.net – Henry Chesbrough's open innovation site.

Paid Content – www.paidcontent.org – new media and digital content.

Project Red Stripe – www.projectredstripe.blogspot.com – The online version of this book.

Rapture – www.youvebeenleftbehind.com – just that.

Spiral Dynamics - www.spiraldynamics.com - your gateway to the theory of everything.

Springwise – www.springwise.com – trend spotting.

TheBrain – www.thebrain.com – visual information management.

Tim O'Reilly – www.oreilly.net – the future of the world wide web.

Twitter – www.twitter.com – social networking and micro-blogging service.

Wrights & Sites – www.mis-guide.com/ws.html – drifting, cities, space, arts, mis-guides: fabulous.

Acknowledgements

Without the Project Red Stripe team, there wouldn't have been a book to write – they were invariably friendly, open and welcoming, answered my questions patiently and always filled me in on what I had missed. They were also admirably able to disregard my scribbling pencil. And they were often much cleverer and much funnier than I've managed to show here.

Without Sally Bibb, who had the idea in the first place, and Mike Seery, who took the brave decision to allow a witness in, no book would have been written.

Without the commitment and support of the late and much lamented Gerard Fairtlough and of Rosie Beckham, Triarchy Press would never have commissioned this book in the first place.

Without the insights of Javier Bajer and Gerard Fairtlough, the book would have been flimsier than a summer negligée of apricot georgette.

Without the gleefully generous teamfulness of my colleagues Alison Melvin, Caroline Milner, Imogen Fallows, Matthew Fairtlough and Tim Heap, I'd've given up somewhere during the last furlong but one.

Without the care and attention of Imogen Fallows, the manuscript would be even more wispily impenetrable than it already is.

Without Maddy, Matthew and Sandra, nothing.

Thank you.

About the Author

Andrew Carey began to emerge in an armoured car during a riot in Singapore in 1956. After a spell as a Senior Inferior, he spent most of his working life helping publishers to commission, edit and sell books, journals, newsletters and magazines. He then trained as a psychotherapist before reverting to type. He makes a tremendous effort to appear nonchalant and likes to be liked.

andrew@triarchypress.com

About Triarchy Press

Triarchy Press is an independent publishing house that looks at how organisations work and how to make them work better. We present challenging perspectives on organisations in short and pithy, but rigorously argued, books.

We have published a number of books by authors who come from a Systems Thinking background. These include: *The Three Ways Of Getting Things Done* by Gerard Fairtlough; *Management F-Laws* by Russell Ackoff, Herb Addison and Sally Bibb; *Systems Thinking in the Public Sector* by John Seddon and *Erasing Excellence* (published in the USA as *Liberating the Schoolhouse*) by Wellford Wilms.

Other titles in the area of innovation include *The Innovation Acid Test* by Andrew Jones and *No Secrets!* by Gerard Fairtlough.

Through our books, pamphlets and website we aim to stimulate ideas by encouraging real debate about organisations in partnership with people who work in them, research them or just like to think about them.

Please tell us what you think about the ideas in this book. Join the discussion at:

www.triarchypress.com/telluswhatyouthink

If you feel inspired to write - or have already written - an article, a pamphlet or a book on any aspect of organisational theory or practice, we'd like to hear from you. Submit a proposal at:

www.triarchypress.com/writeforus

For more information about Triarchy Press, or to order any of our publications, please visit our website or drop us a line:

www.triarchypress.com
info@triarchypress.com

Printed in the United Kingdom
by Lightning Source UK Ltd.
133824UK00001B/385-480/P